遊園尋夢

Wondering
in the dreamland
– The beauty
of Chiang Kai-shek
Memorial Park
中正紀念公園
園林之美

WONDERING
IN THE DREAMLAND
– THE BEAUTY
OF CHIANG KAI-SHEK
MEMORIAL PARK
中正紀念公園
園林之美

目錄　Contents

目錄　Contents

處長序

　　「三十而立」，對中正紀念堂來說，它印證了一個社教館所功能的可塑性。隨著民主政治的進展，中正紀念堂從展示紀念蔣公史蹟的功能不斷提升和擴充，朝向多元化的博物館型態發展，積極推動國際文化交流，提倡藝文風氣，以增進國人藝術人文素養。

　　中正紀念堂除蔣公文物常設展，另設有四個展廳及兩個藝廊，經常舉辦海內外知名藝術家的藝文展覽活動，展出作品從水墨、水彩、攝影、書法、古文物及各類傳統與現代工藝藝術等，展出題材多元豐富，將獨創的藝術作品與文化理念做最完美的呈現。另結合民間資源共同推動國際性、精緻化，且具教育意義的藝文展覽活動，如「金字塔探秘四大古文明--羅浮宮埃及文物展」、「世界恐龍大展」、「蒙娜麗莎的25個秘密─天才達文西特展」等。此外演講廳及教室也提供機關、學校及社團法人等團體，邀請學者、專家辦理富有教育意義的專題演講、研習等活動，皆受到高度歡迎。由於承載特殊歷史意義，並提供多元社教與展覽活動讓國際觀光客大量湧入，中正紀念堂遂成為台北最受歡迎的旅遊景點之一。

　　中正紀念公園亦是充滿自然多樣、生機盎然的生態環境，是許多昆蟲與動物的棲所，只要駐足觀察，就能發現各種生命活潑共存的現象，處處給您驚艷的感受。近年來我們充分運用此人文資源與自然生態環境，營造創意多元的生態及環保園區，孕育出許多生態美景，使民眾毋須跋山涉水，即可親近自然生態。我們更利用這些自然資源，規劃了「數學學習步道」、「自然生態步道」、「定向運動場所」、「雨水貯集再生利用」、「賞鳥、昆蟲步道」等區，提供中小學師生最佳的校外教學園地。而園區四周的迴廊除可遮陽避雨外，更是提供許多社區民眾唱戲、奕棋、運動與休憩的最佳場所，使充滿綠意的紀念園區更增添悠閒情調，同時也拉近了與民眾之間的距離。

　　現在的中正紀念園區不僅是一片綠地、一個公園、更是一座井然有序的動植物大觀園，遂成為台北市最獨特吸引中外遊客造訪的區域。此次我們與中華亞太水彩藝術協會合作，透過藝術家的眼睛，以彩筆描繪此美景，為園區留下紀錄。六十件優美的水彩作品將隨著您一頁一頁的翻閱這本畫集時，呈現在您的眼前，而您也正隨著藝術家的腳步一一的瀏覽園區的各個美景，細品這裡一花一草的丰姿，體會自然之美。

國立中正紀念堂管理處

處長　**曾坤地**　謹誌

2010年10月

Preface

"Establishing at thirty" for Chiang Kai-shek memorial Hall is a confirmation for the adaptability of functions for a social education center. Along with the development of democratic government state, National Chiang Kai-shek memorial hall has elevated and expanded from exhibiting commemorating achievements of Mr. Chiang Kai-shek to a multi-dimensional museum, actively pushing for international cultural exchange, promoting an artistic atmosphere, and increasing the literacy of humanistic cultures of our nation.

Exhibitions other than the possessions of Mr. Chiang Kai-shek have been put on display at the memorial hall as well. At present, there are 4 exhibition halls and 2 art galleries. Collections raging from ink, watercolors, to photography, Chinese calligraphy, and various traditional and modern craftsmanship has demonstrated the dynamic and richness of themes, and a perfect representation of unique artistic creations and cultural ideologies. More international and refined educational exhibitions have been hosted by combining public resources, like the "The Ancient Egyptian Art from Louvre", "Playing with Dinosaurs", and the "Da Vinci the Genius" exhibitions, Furthermore, the auditorium and classrooms provide organizations, schools, and agencies a place to invite scholars and professionals and host eloquent education seminars and lectures, which has become very popular and appreciated. Because the memorial hall has special historical meaning, by organizing dynamic social educational activities and exhibitions, it has attracted a great number of international tourists, thus becoming one of the most popular tourist spots in Taipei.

Chiang Kai-shek memorial park is a vibrant and prosperous ecological environment, home for many insects and animals. If you stop and look carefully, you can discover different energetic lives coexisting together, providing onlookers with the excitement of life. Over the years, we have created an innovative ecological preservation park using the abundant humanistic cultural resources and natural environments around us, producing many spectacles of nature. The public now does not need to travel far to be close to nature. We have further used these natural resources and designed the "Mathematical Travel", "Ecological Trail", "Orienteering zone", "Rainwater recycle system" and "Bird-watching Path", perfect places for outdoor education of elementary and middle schools. The surrounding cloister not only offers a place to hide from the sun and the rain, but also a place for residents to exercise, play chess, and performs Chinese dramas. Because of this, the memorial park has become more relaxing and it has brought people closer to the park.

Apart from being a park and a green field, the current Chiang Kai-shek memorial park is also an organized zoo for animals and plants. This makes it the most distinctive place and attracts tourists from all over the world. Our collaboration with the Asian Watercolor Painting Federation this time has painted its beauty with brushes through the eyes of artists, leaving memoirs for the park. 60 elegant watercolor masterpieces will be showcased right in front of you as you flip through the album page by page. You will be taking a tour in the park with the artists step by step, gracefully appreciating every aspect of it and experience the true beauty of nature.

National Chiang Kai-shek Memorial Hall

Commissioner **Tseng Kun-Ti**

October, 2010

藝術家的眼睛

　　藝術可以是一種包裝也是一種行銷，中正園區絕對值得藝術如此對待，以藝術家的眼睛來發掘，以藝術家的作品來表現，展現中正園區獨特的韻緻和丰采；2010年3月14日，一群中華亞太水彩藝術協會的二十餘位藝術家來到中正園區，他們在園藝組花主任的引導下參訪園區，在讚嘆與驚呼中經歷了一次難忘的生態旅程。在這一個台北版圖中最獨特的園區裡，藝術家開始與自然的對話，以特有的敏感度來搜尋大自然中「美的元素」，無不竭盡所能的進行捕捉影像、感動吸收、儲存醞釀、孕育靈感等；當畫家們回到畫室之中，便將這些已飽吸的靈感激發成動能，經鋪陳結構、揮灑展現至完成作品，將自己融入在那當時豪邁的步履記憶和情境之中，彷彿又再度回到中正園區的情境中，這些作品都是內心澎湃、情緒激動之作。

　　感謝國立中正紀念堂管理處曾坤地處長的支持，這具有多重意義與價值的展覽和專輯同時呈現在讀者眼前。這本由藝術家執筆的專輯有藝術家感性的旅程，以藝術家特有敏銳的眼光捕捉大自然之美，以文字敘述所有旅程中的心境與點滴，還有理性的探索將園中主要常見的動植物以專有名詞之文字和圖版來介紹，加上藝術家的60幅作品創作依序將園區的美景藉由水彩畫特有的美妙韻緻來呈現。

　　中華亞太水彩藝術協會，始終認為藝術必須關懷社會、親近民眾；協會自2005年成立至今，已多次以特定的主題來進行創作，作為激發社會認同與價值思考，期為人類創造更好的生活品質，發揮藝術的社會教育功能；此次中華亞太水彩藝術協會的畫家們，以此為主題進行創作展出，正是一貫的主張，欣賞這些優美的畫作，不需要有高度學習的經歷或長篇大論的文字註解，民眾易於解讀與體會，欣賞畫作沒有壓力、沒有艱澀的難以理解的大抽象；如此藝術擁抱了群眾，群眾亦將會走進藝術。

中華亞太水彩藝術協會理事長

洪東標　謹誌

Eyes of an Artist

Art can be a form of packaging or a form of market, and Chiang Kai-shek Memorial Park is definitely worthy to be treated as such. Discovered through the eyes of artists and presented as a masterpiece, displaying the park's unique flavor and elegant demeanor. On March 14, 2010, more than 20 artists from the Asian Watercolor Association came to Chiang Kai-shek Memorial Park and took a tour with the manager of the Landscaping division. With amazement and praise, they had the most unforgettable ecological trip. In this one of its kind park within Taipei, artists began their conversations with nature, finding different "Elements of beauty" in nature with their own sensitivities, capturing images, absorbing, contemplating, and breeding inspirations. When they head back into their studios, they transform these stimulations into active energy, constructing and wielding it into works of art. Bringing themselves back into the memories and environments of their moving walk, they seem to be back within the park, and all these paintings are the creations of their expressive and moving self.

We thank Commissioner Tseng Kun Ti of the National Chiang Kai-shek memorial Hall for all his support in presenting this valuable and meaningful exhibition and album to the readers. This sentimental journey written through the keen eyes of artists shows the simple beauty of nature, with words describing details and the their state of mind throughout. It also sensibly investigates and introduces the main commonly seen animals and plants in their professional names and pictures. Moreover, the 60 watercolor masterpieces drawn by the artists chronologically showcase the exquisiteness of the park.

The Asian Watercolor Painting Federation believes that art should be about giving back to the society and reaching out to the public. Since its establishment in 2005, we have created many works of art in specific themes, hoping to gain society approval and values. Our goal is to create a better living quality for humans and exercise the social education function of art. Artists that are part of the Asian Watercolor Painting Federation has presented art based on this idea and we believe that appreciating these beauties does not require extensive education or long commentaries. The public can understand and experience them without pressure and the incomprehensible abstract content. Such art has embraced the public, thus the public shall walk into its arms.

Asian Watercolor Painting Federation
Chairman Mr. Hung Tung-Piao

Hung Tung Piao

WONDERING
IN THE DREAMLAND
- THE BEAUTY
OF CHIANG KAI-SHEK
MEMORIAL PARK
中正紀念公園
園林之美

遊園尋夢

暢遊花叢綠園，尋覓生態幽夢

台北盆地的繁華，匯聚了你和我，
路上車水馬龍，街巷人群穿梭，
在忙忙碌碌的日子裡，
總是期待，
可以享受片刻的悠閒灑脫。

中正紀念公園，用心為您圓夢，
如今花草林木綠意盎然，動物前來共享盛宴，
這片闊土，變成了都會綠寶石，
散發出迷人的丰采！

誠摯邀您，
一同暢遊花叢綠園，尋覓生態幽夢。

讓
遍地的青草、繽紛的花彩，
拭亮您疲憊的雙眸。

清淨的湖水，
沉澱心中交錯的煩憂。

桂花的淡香，
舒緩著平日急促的吸吐。

櫻花梅花的盛開，
激起聲聲的驚嘆。

杉木林道的沁涼綠蔭，
讓那緊迫無歇的節奏，
尋回久違輕鬆的步伐！

闔上雙眼，
輕聞
葉的氣息、花的香！
聆聽
鳥語、蟬鳴、蛙唱……

微風
拂起衣袖，吹涼雙頰，
撥動了漣漪的琴弦，
邀約群樹一同呢喃輕唱！

為自己，
留張白紙吧！
鋪上了水，沾滿了彩，
揮灑出　繁花盛開的燦麗，
渲染著　草綠天藍的壯闊！
用筆描繪，與松鼠邂逅的悸動，
用心刻劃，發現紅冠水雞的欣喜！
…………
與大自然　一次次的相遇，
為心靈　寫下一篇篇的浪漫與輕柔。

Wondering in the Dreamland
Visit the green garden and find the ecological beauty of your dreams

The prosperity of the Taipei basin makes us all come together
Heavy traffic on the road, crowds walking on the street,
in busy days like these
we all expect
to instantly enjoy the leisurely and carefree moments.

Chiang Kai-shek Memorial Park
is doing the best to make your dream come true.
This land is now covered with greenery and beautiful flowers
It is a land, where animals become our guests of grand banquet
It is a land that becomes the emerald of the city,
shining and charming.

We sincerely invite you to visit this green garden
and find the ecological beauty of your dreams

Let verdant grass and riotous flowers on the earth
to shine in to your fatigued eyes

The tranquil and crystal lake
will sweep millions of worries all away.

The smell of sweet osmanthus
will smooth your rapid and short breaths

The blossom of sakura and plum flowers
will bring exclamations of praise

The freshness of the China fir forest
will turn the pressing and restless tempo
back to a long-ago relaxing pace!

Close your eyes
And smell~
the freshness of leaves and the sweetness of flowers
Then listen~
to the orchestra of birds, cicadas and frogs…

The wind blows~
lifts sleeves and chills our faces
It then blows across the water and slides the strings,
inviting trees to sing altogether

Let's leave a blank piece of paper
for yourself.
Spread water over the paper and touch some colors
Brush the beauty of flower blossom
And paint the immensity of green grass and blue sky
Use your pen to record the touching moment of meeting squirrels
And use your heart to remember the joy of discovering common moorhen…

Every each time you meet the beautiful nature
will bring unlimited tenderness and imagination
to your spirit and mind.

WONDERING
IN THE DREAMLAND
—THE BEAUTY
OF CHIANG KAI-SHEK
MEMORIAL PARK
中正紀念公園
園林之美

綠臂彎
城市中的綠色臂彎

中正紀念公園位於台北市的樞紐，
佔地約有二十五公頃。
寬厚的綠帶　由紀念堂的後方，
沿著兩側連結至兩廳院，
形如臂膀，庭園綠意盎然，叢林濃密蓊鬱，
隔離了城市的喧囂。

園區特地栽種了不同地區、氣候的樹種，
光是台灣原生植物，就有二百多種。
更精心規劃了許多主題區塊：
多肉植物區、香草植物區、蘭花雨林區、
蕨類植物區、觀賞鳳梨區、球根植物區、
天南星科植物區、虎背生態教學區、藥用植物區、
竹芋科植物區、櫻花區、梅花區……等，
散發著植物多樣的魅力與風情。

水池的清澈、花草林木的豐富，
孕育出美好的生態環境，
吸引了許多動物前來覓食、築巢定居、繁殖後代；
當您漫步於林園湖畔時，
松鼠、攀木蜥蜴、喜鵲、黑冠麻鷺、紅冠水雞……，
總會與您不期而遇，
如此微妙的邂逅，是驚亦是喜！

搭乘捷運，抵達中正紀念堂，
步出5號出口，經過國家戲劇院，
您將進入"城市裡的綠色臂彎"中！
這兒近在咫尺，
無需舟車勞頓之苦，
即可擁抱親吻大自然，
沐浴在鳥語花香的氛圍中，
那是城市人夢想已久的奢華與享受呀！

園區不斷地努力，
營造一片充滿生命的都會生態公園，
為市民提供運動、休憩、觀光、教學的好去處，
這是屬於你和我的大花園！

Green Arms
The city's green arms

Chang Kai-shek Memorial Park is located at the hub of Taipei City,
Covering approximately 25 hectares.
The wide, thick green belt begins at the back of the Memorial Hall,
And connects along the sides to the National Theater Concert Hall
Like arms. The garden, green and luxuriant,
Segregates the city noise.

The Park planted trees from different areas and climates,
With Taiwanese plants alone adding to more than 200 varieties.
In addition, the park has carefully planned many theme areas:
Succulents Garden, Aromatic and Herbal Plants Garden, Orchid Rainforest Garden,
Pteridophyta Garden, Bromeliaceae Garden, Bulbs Garden,
Araceae Garden, Hubei Ecological Education District, Taiwan's Herb Garden,
Marantaceae Plant Garden, Cherry Garden, Plum Area……,
Displaying the many charms and expressions of plants.

The clarity of ponds and luxuriance of plants
Breed an exquisite ecological environment,
Attracting many animals to come seek food, build nests and reproduce;
When you stroll along the lakeside,
Squirrels, Suinhoe's japaluras, Magpies, Malay Night Heron, Moorhens…
Come to greet you unexpectedly.
A delicate and surprising encounter!

Take the MRT to Chang Kai-shek Memorial Hall,
Step out exit 5, pass through National Theater,
And you will enter the "city's green arms!"
It is near,
Saving you from the trouble of traveling wearily
To embrace nature
And bathe in an aura of bird songs and floral fragrance.
A long-yearned luxury and enjoyment of city people!

The park continues to strive
To create a lively metropolitan ecological park,
To provide citizens with a good place to exercise, rest, tour and educate.
This is a big garden that belongs to you and me!

中山南路
Zhongshan S. RD

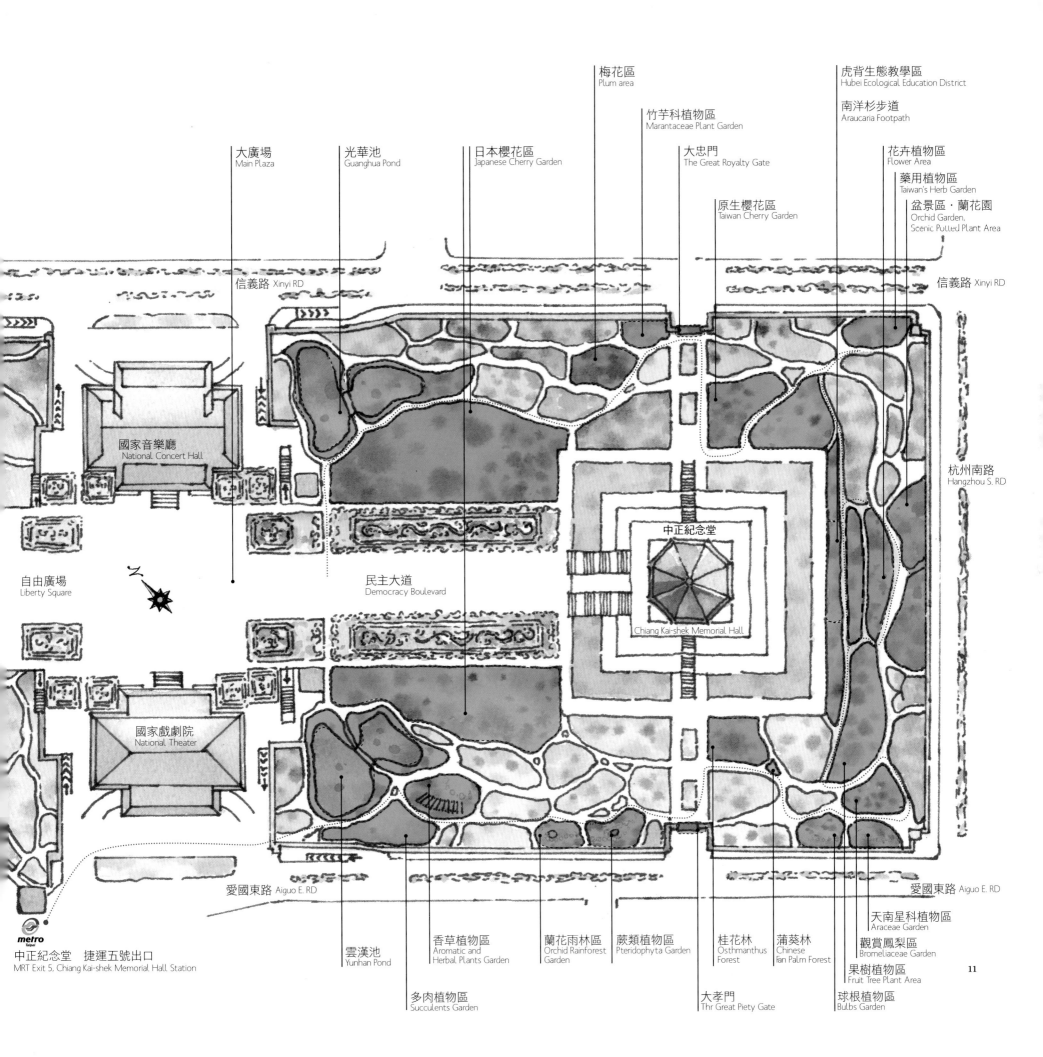

大廣場
Main Plaza

光華池
Guanghua Pond

日本櫻花區
Japanese Cherry Garden

梅花區
Plum area

竹芋科植物區
Marantaceae Plant Garden

大忠門
The Great Royalty Gate

原生櫻花區
Taiwan Cherry Garden

虎背生態教學區
Hubei Ecological Education District

南洋杉步道
Araucaria Footpath

花卉植物區
Flower Area

藥用植物區
Taiwan's Herb Garden

盆景區・蘭花園
Orchid Garden,
Scenic Potted Plant Area

信義路 Xinyi RD

信義路 Xinyi RD

國家音樂廳
National Concert Hall

中正紀念堂
Chiang Kai-shek Memorial Hall

杭州南路
Hangzhou S. RD

自由廣場
Liberty Square

民主大道
Democracy Boulevard

國家戲劇院
National Theater

愛國東路 Aiguo E. RD

愛國東路 Aiguo E. RD

metro
Taipei

中正紀念堂　捷運五號出口
MRT Exit 5, Chiang Kai-shek Memorial Hall Station

雲漢池
Yunhan Pond

香草植物區
Aromatic and
Herbal Plants Garden

多肉植物區
Succulents Garden

蘭花雨林區
Orchid Rainforest
Garden

蕨類植物區
Pteridophyta Garden

桂花林
Osthmanthus
Forest

大孝門
Thr Great Piety Gate

蒲葵林
Chinese
fan Palm Forest

球根植物區
Bulbs Garden

天南星科植物區
Araceae Garden

觀賞鳳梨區
Bromeliaceae Garden

果樹植物區
Fruit Tree Plant Area

11

雲漢池

映著天藍，映著樹綠，也映了心……

雲漢池，
形如葫蘆，池中橫跨著潔白的拱橋，
池邊大樹圍繞，
肯式南洋杉、榕樹、茄苳、垂柳、緬梔花……，
枝葉扶疏、蓊鬱濃密，
為池畔帶來沁涼幽靜。

繁忙的您，
讓紛亂起伏的思緒與煩惱，
訴諸這片池水，
在水平線上，尋回寧靜。
水靜如鏡，
映著天藍、映著樹綠、也映了心，
映出那久別的寬鬆與歡欣……。

夜鷺佇立在榕樹上乘涼，
時而梳理毛羽，時而望著池面發呆。
圓圓的小浮板，是巴西龜的日光浴廣場；
池中小島，是紅冠水雞家人的幸福天地，
小島上長滿了水生植物，
在灰藍的水面上，格外鮮明美麗。

那天，
步上了拱橋，欣賞水中的白雲，
突然，吹來一陣涼風！
哇，
小島，竟然漂遊旋轉了起來！
夢幻奇妙的情境，
彷彿置身於神話卡通般！
抽個空，帶孩子過來走走吧！
當十元硬幣投進大紅鯉魚的機器肚裡，
他睜大期待的雙眼，盯著那罐飼料噗地掉出來！
孩子興奮極了！

牽著他的小手，一同坐在池邊，
當一把把的飼料撒出，
哇！
媽咪！媽咪！魚好多、好大、好漂亮呀！（錦鯉、吳郭魚）
那邊有烏龜耶！（巴西龜）
爸比！紅嘴鳥的一家人也游過來吃飼料了！（紅冠水雞）
……
聲聲開懷的驚呼，為童年留下許多美好的回憶！

【雲漢池：池名取自明監國魯王朱以海手書之「漢影雲根」】

Yunhan Pond

Reflecting the blue of the sky, green of the trees, and the heart...

Yunhan Pond
Shaped like a calabash, a pure white arch bridge stretched across
Surrounded by prominent trees,
Moreton Bay Pine, Chinese Banyan, Autumn maple tree, Weeping Willow,
Temple Tree...
Branches and leaves are luxuriant,
Bringing a cool, peaceful air to the bank of the pond

Busy as you are,
Let your tangled thoughts and worries
Be freed by this pond of water.
And find serenity at the water horizon.
The water, still as a mirror,
Reflects the blue of the sky, the green of the trees, and the heart,
Reflecting those long forgotten senses of relaxation and delight.

A Black-crowned Night Heron stands on the branches of the Chinese
Banyan, cooling off,
At times combing its feathers, at times staring blankly at the pond.
A Red-ear Turtle is sun bathing on a small, round float board.
The Moorhen family is enjoying their time on the little island
in the middle of the pond.
The island, full of aquatic plants,
Is exceptionally vivid and beautiful on the grey blue water surface.

That day,
Stepping onto the arch bridge to admire white clouds in the water,
And suddenly, a cool breeze!
Wow!
The island, revolving!
A dreamy and fantastical scene,
As though placed in a mythical cartoon!
Find time to bring the kids here!
When a $10 coin was inserted into the big red Koi's mechanical belly,
His eyes opened wide in expectation, for the can of fodder to come falling down!
The kid was extremely excited!

Holding his tiny hand, we sat together by the pond,
And when handfuls of fodder were dispensed,
Wow!
Mommy! Mommy! So many fish and so big, so beautiful! (Colored Carp,Tilapia)
A turtle! (Red-ear Turtle)
Daddy! The red-mouthed bird's family
is swimming over to eat the fodder! (Moorhen)
...
Cheerful exclamations, leaving behind many wonderful childhood memories.

(Yunhan Pond: The pond's name is derived from Han Ying Yun Gen handwritten by
Southern Ming Dynasty Emperor Prince Lu Zhu Yihai)

WONDERING
IN THE DREAMLAND
– THE BEAUTY
OF CHIANG KAI-SHEK
MEMORIAL PARK
中正紀念公園
園林之美

巴西龜
學名: *Trachemys scripta elegans*
正確名稱為紅耳泥龜，眼後有明顯紅斑，其食量很大，適
應力強，在臺灣已嚴重威脅到本土龜類的生存。屬於雜食
性，飼料、魚蝦、蔬菜水果等都吃，雌龜大於雄龜，每年產
2-5窩蛋，每窩約10-15顆左右，在90天左右孵化，幼龜體色
翠綠十分可愛，廣受世界各國大量引進，巴西龜需經常做
日光浴，有高度群居性，在園區兩魚池皆可見到其蹤跡，
每年春夏交替之間，亦可見到牠們上岸產卵的景象。

Red-ear turtle
Scientific name: *Trachemys scripta elegans*
The correct name of this kind of turtle is Red-ear Turtle,
it has obvious red spot behind the eyes; the food quantity
required is in great amount. With high adaptability for
surviving, it has already threatened seriously the existence
of local turtles. The Red-ear turtle is omnivorous, for
example, feed, fish, shrimp, vegetable and fruit. The female
turtle is larger than the male one; they breed usually 2-5
broods yearly with 10-15 eggs each time, the eggs would
hatch in about 90 days, the delicate and lovely kid turtles
are widely introduced by various countries. As a highly
social animal, Brazilian Slider, needs a lot of sunshine; they
are frequently seen in the two ponds of garden. During
the spring and summer season exchanging period, Red-ear
turtle habitually laid eggs on the riverbank.

夜鷺
學名: *Nycticorax nycticorax*
夜鷺的俗名為暗光鳥或暗光，表示牠是夜行性的水鳥，多在晨
昏、夜晚出來捕食，以獵捕魚蝦、兩棲類、昆蟲為主，在繁殖期
為了育雛也會白天出來覓食。飛行常會發出『呱-呱-呱』的粗
啞鳴聲。成鳥全身呈灰藍色系，如果看到大小相當而全身灰褐
色，帶著白色斑點的水鳥，不要以為是不知名的另一種鳥，牠
其實是夜鷺的亞成鳥啦。

Black-crowned Night Heron
Scientific name: *Nycticorax nycticorax*
The popular name of Night Heron is Dark Light Bird or Dark
Light, implying it is a nocturnal animal. They usually forage in
the early morning and during the nighttime, mainly hunting for
fishes, shrimps, amphibians, and insects, but sometimes they
can be found during the daytime finding food for breeding
the nestlings. The Night Heron make a coarse sound as "gua-
gua-gua" while flying. The adult birds are all gray-blue; if
you happen to see a gray-brown waterbird with white spots
of almost the same size with Night Heron, it is not any bird
without a name, it's actually the sub-adult bird of Night Heron.

錦鯉

學名: *Cyprinus carpio*

錦鯉是具有色彩和斑紋，飼養來做觀賞的鯉魚。牠具有觀賞性且可長時間持有。以觀賞的觀點，依照其斑紋及鱗的狀態區分十三個品種，而以紅白、大正三色、昭和三色為最基本的，錦鯉與其他魚不同之處乃在牠的底色為白色，鮮明美麗，唯有昭和三色，底為黑色。這三種錦鯉不同於其他錦鯉，其餘十種均為雜交而產出。錦鯉是以其花紋特色交配，將其花紋遺傳特性相互交雜，產生無數品種，目前主要品種約有一百多種。

Colored Carp

Scientific name: *Cyprinus carpio*

The Colored Carp is a fish with various colors and stripes, they are generally bred for seeing and enjoying, its unique beauty lasts normally for quite long time. If categorized by stripes and scales, they can be divided into 13 kinds of breeds, while red-white, Taisho Sanke koi and Showa three color koi are three basic kinds. The difference between Variegated Carp and other fishes is, the ground color of former is remarkably beautiful white, while Showa three color koi is the only one with black ground color. Different from other tens kind of Variegated Carp continue their next generation by hybridizing, the mating of aforesaid three unique kinds are based on stripes, producing multi-breeds through crossing the specific stripes inherited, there are over 100 different breeds currently.

WONDERING
IN THE DREAMLAND
– THE BEAUTY
OF CHIANG KAI-SHEK
MEMORIAL PARK
中正紀念公園
園林之美

緬槴花
學名: *Plumeria rubra* L

別名雞蛋花、印度素馨、蛋黃花，葉互生，簇生於枝條頂端，長橢圓形，兩端尖銳，冬季落葉。花頂生，聚繖花序，花冠五裂迴旋排列，一般常見為外部乳白，內部鮮黃，極似去殼的雞蛋，故又名雞蛋花。具芳香，春末到夏季盛開，亦有整朵為黃色、粉紅或濃紅色的品種。樹姿、花朵優美，是美化庭園的好樹種。日照需充足，耐旱抗鹼，性喜高溫，全株具乳汁，有毒。園區目前白色及濃紅色兩種花色。

Temple Tree
Scientific name: *Plumeria rubra* L

The Egg Flower, Plumeria acutifolia and Egg Yolk Flower are its trivial names. The leaf of this plant is long and oval-shaped, pointed at two ends, alternate phyllotaxy clustered at the top of branch, falls in winter time. Flower terminal, compound dichasium, 5 sympetalous, in circle formed; generally in creamy color exteriorly, and bright yellow interiorly, extremely resembling to a shelled egg, which is also the origin of its popular name, Egg Flower. The fragrant flower blossoms from the end of spring and the whole summer, the breeds of pure yellow, pink, or intense red can be sometimes seen. The elegant form of tree and delicacy of flower make it broadly favored by garden beautification. The Egg Flower needs lots of sunshine and prefers high temperature environment, with characteristics as dry-resistance and anti-alkali, besides, its poisonous latex contained in the whole plant. There are current white and intense red Temple Tree cultivated in the garden.

茄苳
學名: *Bischofia jabanica* Blume.

又名重陽木、加冬、紅桐、秋楓樹、烏陽、胡楊，樹幹粗糙不平，常會有瘤狀的突起，赤褐色樹皮，會有層狀剝落。葉為三出複葉，互生，新葉紅褐色。圓錐花序，花黃色，極小。果實未成熟時是青綠色，成熟時則為褐色，有如一串串葡萄掛在枝頭，極為壯觀，也可以拿來醃製成漬物，味道甘甜甜的。茄苳是原生樹種，分佈在低海拔地區。長成高大的樹木時，樹冠為傘狀，極具有遮陰效果，為優良的行道樹(仁愛路即是)。常見的老樹中有四大天王，那就是榕樹、樟樹、茄苳和楓香。

Autumn maple tree
Scientific name: *Bischofia jabanica* Blume.

The Chinese Bishopwood, Tong Tree, Red Cedar, Autumn Maple Tree, Dark Sun Tree, and Java Bishopwood are several local names of Bishop Wood. Many protruding spines can be found on its rough trunk, and the red-brown bark peels off layer after layer. Ternate compound leaf, alternate phyllotaxy, the new leaf is red-brown, and the yellow, extremely small flower is in panicle inflorescence. The fruits are verdure before maturity, then turns to brown afterwards, they look as if numerous strings of grapes hanging on the branches, the view is quite splendid. The fruits are sometimes preserved as candied food, the taste is soft and sweet. Bishop Wood is Taiwan Nato tree, located in the low altitude area. The grown up tree is very tall, and the umbrella shaped tree-crown creates a shady and cool place under the blazing sun; it is deemed an excellent choice for shade tree (e.g., Jen-ai Road). The banyan, camphor tree, Chinese sweet gum and Bishop Wood are the four kings among the frequently seen old trees.

紅冠水雞
學名: *Gallinula chloropus*

俗名紅雞、黑水雞，全身為黑褐色，嘴為明顯的紅色、先端黃色，額部有紅色斑塊，腳為黃綠色，腳爪趾相當細長，能在水面水草上行走自如，且擅於游泳。雛鳥全身烏黑，額頭有鮮明之紅點。為普遍易見的留鳥，生活於池塘、湖泊、沼澤地等溼地環境或河邊植物叢中。屬雜食性鳥類，主食水草、植物嫩芽及水生昆蟲、軟體動物等。本園區兩魚池皆可見到其蹤跡。每年3~7月是牠們的繁殖期，可見到母雞帶著小雞覓食的可愛模樣。

Moorhen
Scientific name: *Gallinula chloropus*

Red Chicken and Dark Water Chicken are the popular names of Gallinula chloropus. This kind of fowl is all black-brown, with noticeable red beak, the front is yellow, and some red spots on neck, the yellow-green feet have long claws, so it can walk on water easily and is skilled at swimming. The young bird is all black with red spots on the neck. They are commonly birds, and usually live in the wetlands such as pond, lake, and swamp as well as brushwood along the riverbank. Moorhen is omnivorous, waterweeds, shoot of vegetables, water insects and malacostracan are their major foods. They are regularly seen in the fish pond of this garden; during the breed period, usually from March to July, the mother chicken would take her cute little ones out for foraging around.

鄧國強　紅冠水雞　36×56cm　2010
深綠的樹叢為背景，讓白色的拱橋明顯突出，白橋
的倒影，在微風吹動的水中搖晃不定。右下側的紅
冠水雞是主題，我特地將它拉近放大，來向讀者介
紹這隻在都市中難得一見的珍禽。

Teng Kuo-Chiang　Moorhen
Set against the background of the dark green tree bushes, it highlights the white arched bridge, and the reflection of the white bridge on the water glimmers amid the gentle breeze. The Moorhen at the lower right was the subject, which I purposely enlarged it to introduce to the readers the precious moorhen rarely seen in the city.

遊園尋夢

WONDERING
IN THE DREAMLAND
- THE BEAUTY
OF CHIANG KAI-SHEK
MEMORIAL PARK
園林之美

林毓修　春意催　56×76cm　2010

Lin Yu-Hsiu　Pressing Spring

上一季還來不及凋盡的秋葉，落得讓滿池的翠綠…絕
美到令人心醉。池畔的杜鵑也不甘勢弱地恣意綻放，
宣誓著季節的地盤，桃紅、粉白、飽滿欲滴。一旁如
繁星般飛舞的花白，也在一抹黛綠中跳躍著。對映水
面上新冒的嫩綠、如樂曲般起伏有致；更是強迫攻佔
你的視野。
當水鳥優雅地游過池面，便串起這一池生命的驚喜與
感動。才驚覺…"春"已悄悄來到了雲漢池！

The late withered leaves of last autumn fell in all over the green pond…enchants everyone by its sadly beauty.
The rhododendrons around the pond splendidly bloom as if announcing the territory of season; the pinkish and pink-white flowers gracefully show their charm.Beside then are some white flowers, dance as naughty sprites in a dark green; by contrast, the new emerged tender leaves ripple on water as if music notes, confidently attracting all your attention for its splendid view.
When water bird gracefully swims across the pond, connecting all the surprise and emotion of lives in pond; till that moment did I realize that "spring" has already arrived quietly at Yunhan pond.

李招治　慈暉　55×75cm　2010

紅冠水雞在中正紀念堂的雲漢池築巢育雛，隱在一片
翠綠中，小寶寶依偎著親鳥，有親愛有依賴。大自然
隨時隨地不在訴説著生息百態；呈現生命的內涵；訴
説生命的啟示，畫中想説的正是如此。

Li Zhao-zhi　Caring Love

In the Yunhan Pond of the National Chiang Kai-shek Memorial Hall, the Moorhen build nest for breeding the little ones. They hide in an entire jade green, with love and dependence, the babies cling to their parent. The Nature tells always the incredible sides of Lives, showing the meaning of life and describing the revelation of life, which is exactly this painting intends to express.

多肉植物區

堅強不屈　極簡極美

位於雲漢池右側，靠近愛國東路，
有一處小沙丘，
遍地爬滿著紫花綠葉的馬鞍藤，
沙丘上的植物，沒有枝葉交錯的濃密，
反而開闊明亮、一覽無遺，
這兒就是多肉植物區。

仙人掌、皇冠龍舌蘭、金虎、酒瓶蘭……，
一棵棵佇立在乾燥的沙地上，
有的如球如柱、有的如扇如掌，簡單厚實，
荒涼中，帶著幾分莊嚴與傲氣，
走在其中，有如置身於海邊或沙漠中！

是命運注定、或是自己的抉擇，
多肉植物世世代代，
生長在乾旱炎熱、或寒冷、或高鹽度的環境中。
它們接受了土地的貧瘠，氣候的惡劣，
學習適應，演化自己，
捨盡植物原有的嬌柔飄逸，
將一身蛻化成樸素簡約。

但，簡樸的它，
竟開出了無比燦麗的花朵！
是種母愛吧，
自己如此克勤克儉，
卻讓最美好的，全給了下一代！

"堅強不屈""極簡極美"的生命哲學，
讓多肉植物在艱辛的環境中，
依然可以如此怡然自得，
您是否也感受到這股非凡的氣魄呢！

Succulents Garden

Strong and unbending, minimal and exquisite

Located on the right side of the Yunhan Pond, near Aiguo E. RD.,
A small sand dune,
Is covered with the purple and green of Railroad Vine.
Plants on the dune are not luxuriant with interlacing branches and leaves,
But open and bright, all to be taken in at a glance.
This is the Succulents Garden.

Cactuses, Crown Agaves, Dwarf Hollies, Ponytail...
Stand on dry sand land.
Some are like balls and pillars; others resemble fans and palms,
simple and solid,
Carrying an air of dignity and arrogance in the bleakness.
To walk within is like being at the sea or desert!

Destined by fate, or chosen by free will,
Generations of succulent plants
Have grown on arid and hot, or cold, or highly salty environments.
They have accepted the barren land, the abominable climate
And have learned to adapt and evolve,
Forsaking the frail nature of plants
To morph into simplicity

But, simple as it is,
Flourishes with resplendent flowers!
It is a kind of motherly love,
Practicing frugality,
Only to give the best to the next generation!

Applying the life philosophies of "strong and unbending" and "minimal and beautiful"
In difficult environments,
Have allowed succulent plants to stay at peace.
Do you also sense the extraordinary vigor?

WONDERING
IN THE DREAMLAND
– THE BEAUTY
OF CHIANG KAI-SHEK
MEMORIAL PARK
中正紀念公園
園林之美

多肉植物

在園藝學上把一些肥厚多汁的植物，統稱為多肉植物，包含「仙人掌」與「其他多肉植物」，如仙人掌科、景天科、番杏科、大戟科、百合科、蘿藦科、龍舌蘭科、菊科、夾竹桃科、馬齒莧科、瓜科及唇形科等等。這類植物具有肥厚多汁的肉質莖、葉或根，大部分生長在乾旱或一年中有一段時間乾旱的地區，因此演化出具有發達的薄壁組織以貯藏水分。

多肉植物的原生環境主要是沙漠及海岸地區，除仙人掌類的分布局限於美洲外，廣泛分布在世界各地的乾旱地區或乾燥環境，但數量及種類還是以非洲和美洲最多。台灣雖氣候多雨，但在西部地區冬季卻有數個月的乾季，因此也有原生的多肉植物，包括有景天科的1種八寶屬（Hylotelephium）、3種燈籠草屬（Kalanchoe）和14種佛甲草屬（Sedum）植物。另在一些鹽沼地區，亦有藜科、馬齒莧科和番杏科的鹽生性多肉植物分布。

Succulent Plants

In horticulture, plants with succulent juices are generally called succulent plants, including cactuses and other succulent plants such as Cactaceae, Crassulaceae, Aizoaceae, Euphorbiaceae, Liliaceae, Asclepiadaceae, Agavaceae, Asteraceae, Apocynaceae, Portulacaceae, Caricaceae, Lamiaceae and so on. These plants have succulent stems, leaves or roots, and most grown in arid regions or regions with arid periods during the year, thus evolving into highly developed structures capable of water storage. Succulent plants have originally grown in deserts and coastal areas. Other than cactuses which are mostly limited to the Americas, succulent plants are widely seen in arid regions or dry environments around the world, though the Americas and Africa still have the most quantities and varieties. Although Taiwan has a rainy climate, it has several months of dryness during the winter in the western area, hence it also has local succulent plants, including in the Crassulaceae family,1 variety of the Hylotelephium, 3 varieties of the Kalanchoe and 14 varieties of the Sedum. In some salt marshes, there are also Chenopodiaceae, Portulacaceae and Aizoaceae which grow in salty environments.

馬鞍藤
學名: *Ipomoea pes-caprae* subsp. *brasiliensis*

又名厚藤、鱟藤、馬蹄藤、二葉紅蕃，馬鞍藤因葉片先端凹裂，形狀如馬鞍而得名。仔細看它的花朵，與我們所熟知的牽牛花極為相似，它們同屬旋花科牽牛屬的成員，馬鞍藤是典型的沙灘植物，通常是沙岸最前線的植物群落，耐鹽又耐高鹼性土壤，因長期生長在空曠的海濱沙灘上或河邊堤防上，莖不像牽牛花能纏繞攀緣，而是匍匐蔓生，極力向四面八方拓展地盤。花朵壽命很短，清晨綻放，過中午就凋謝，想欣賞其繁花盛開的景致，一定要記得早上去欣賞哦！

Seahore Vine Morning Glory
Scientific name: *Ipomoea pes-caprae* subsp. *brasiliensis*

The Seahore Vine Morning Glory has several local names, such as thick vine, horse foot vine, saddle vine, two-leaf red vine. The name of saddle vine originated from the crack at the top front of its leaf, the fractured shape looks like a horse saddle. The flower of the Seahore Vine Morning Glory highly resembles the Morning Glory if we observe it carefully; in fact, both of them are Convolvulaceae, Ipomoea. The Seahore Vine Morning Glory is a typical beach plant, resistant against salt and high alkali soil, usually grows in clusters on the top frontline of sand beach. the Seahore Vine Morning Glory does not wind around or climb as Morning Glory, instead, this trailing plant expands utmost its territory towards every directions, since it grows in a spacious area or along the river dike. The lifespan of flower is very short, it blooms in the morning, then withers right after the noon, so remember to appreciate the beauty of blossom in the morningl

皇冠龍舌蘭

皇冠龍舌蘭
學名: *Agave attenuata* 'Nerva'

屬多年生草本的大型多肉植物，全株呈半球形，因類似皇冠而得名。葉叢狀集生，葉片肉質，表面革質，闊披針形，葉緣鋸齒狀，呈放射狀生長，先端及葉緣均具有銳刺，觀賞時要小心，不要被其刺傷了！老株生長十數年後會開花，花梗上能萌生許多個芽體，待芽體葉片長出數片後，再剪下扦插，成活後就是另外一個新的生命，此法可大量繁殖小苗。

Crown Agave
Scientific name: *Agave attenuata* 'Nerva'

A perennial, large succulent plant. The stem is a semi-circle, resembling a crown, which gives the plant its name. The leaves are ovate-acumimnate, succulent and leathery smooth, have saw-tooth edges and grow in a radial form. The tip and edges of the leaves bear sharp thorns, so be careful not to get pricked. The old embryo has flower blossoms after a decade or more, and the flower stems produce individual sprouts. When the sprout leaves have grown several leaves, it can be used to grow another new life; the method can reproduce sprouts in large quantities.

龍舌蘭

酒瓶蘭
學名: *Nolina recurvata* (Lem.) Hemsley

又名酒矸蘭、酒磅蘭，莖幹直立，下部肥大，形狀像酒瓶而得名，老株表皮呈粗糙龜裂，狀似龜甲，其肥大圓幹莖具有肥厚的木栓層樹皮。葉叢生，單葉，呈線形，自然下垂，葉端漸尖，全緣，葉面平滑，革質，無葉柄。圓錐花序，在全日照下成熟植株才會開花。成熟植株適合庭園栽植，幼株適合盆栽，可放置室內觀賞，生長速度極為緩慢。

Ponytail
Scientific name: *Nolina recurvata* (Lem.) Hemsley

Also called Wine Flask. it has an erect trunk with a plump base, getting its name from resembling the shape of a wine flask. The bark is rough and cracked, like a tortoise shell, and the plump bark base produces thick cork cambium. The leaf grows in clumps and is a simple leaf (undivided blade) with a linear line which droops downwards, becoming pointier towards the tip. The leaf surface is smooth like leather and has no leafstalk. The flowers are in a panicle, and need full sun to flourish. The mature embryo is suitable for growing in gardens, while the shoots are suitable for Bonsai to be admired indoors. It grows extremely slowly.

WONDERING
IN THE DREAMLAND
- THE BEAUTY
OF CHIANG KAI-SHEK
MEMORIAL PARK
中正紀念公園
園林之美

柯衛光　仙境
39.4×27.3cm　2010
作畫前，來一次深度遊園，到多肉植物區，
頭頂出現？！同伴們道：「啥時中正紀念堂
有這麼多仙人掌」。本以為只有我一人『無
知』，確有多數人不知。
如果您也未發現，有興趣來一趟「仙人掌之
境」

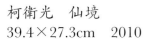

Ke Wei-guang　Fairyland
Before starting painting, I made a deep
exploration in garden; when I came to the
succulents Garden...what is that up there?
Someone said, "Since when the National Chiang
Kai-shek Memorial Hall got so many cacti?
"Well, so I'm not the only "innocent" one.
If you have not yet found this amazing place,
it is worth paying a visit to the "cacti land".

郭心漪　大戟麒麟　56×56cm　2010　Kuo Hsin-i　Crown of Thorns Euphorbia
就算是全株都有劇毒並一身刺甲，還是不減它散發出
的獨特美感。

Even the whole plant is lethally poisonous and entirely covered with thorns, the unique beauty of this plant is not least lessened.

香草植物區
香味，是"回憶的小精靈"

穿過數棵肯式南洋杉，順著白色花架的引領，
即可徜徉在植物的芳香氛圍中~香草植物區。

香味，是"回憶的小精靈"，
它頑皮地在腦海中，翻閱著一章章的浪漫故事！

香茅草，是否讓您想起保護您的防蚊液呢？
涼爽的薄荷，帶來口齒的清香！
九層塔，追憶著母親做的滑溜煎蛋與蛤蜊湯，
迷迭香，令人懷念起民宿主人特地煎烤的迷迭雞......！

第一次約會，微風中飄逸著她淡淡的髮香，
小baby身上的臭奶香、以及洗完澎澎後皮膚的嫩香，
熬夜讀書，窗外飄來的夜來香與柚子花香，
還有那帶您甜睡入夢的被窩香，
以及讓您愉悅溫馨的家庭香......！

啊！
誘人的植物香，無時無刻瀰漫在生活中，
吸引了味蕾、嗅覺......迷戀著、陶醉著！
它串起一齣齣的美好記憶......，
好讓閒暇之餘，
輕輕翻閱、慢慢回味......。

Aromatic and Herbal Plants Garden

Scent, was "elf memories"

Willing to type the number of trees through the hoop pine
along the white flower of the lead,
Aromatic plants can roam in the atmosphere ~
Aromatic and Herbal Plants Garden.

Flavor is the "memory of the little wizard",
It is naughty in mind, read a chapter by chapter of the romantic story!

Lemongrass, if you remember your mosquito repellant to protect it?
Cool mint, bringing articulate the fragrance!
Basil, recalling her mother's slippery omelette made with clam soup
Rosemary, is nostalgic for the proprietor,
specifically the rosemary grilled chicken ... ...!

First date, her faint breeze flowing hair fragrance
Little baby smell milky body, and after washing the skin soft
and smelling good,
Stay up all night reading the window blown Tuberose floral and grapefruit,
Sleeping dreams are that the blanket with your fragrance,
And make your home pleasant and warm incense ... ...!

Ah!
Attractive plant incense filled in life all the time,
To attract the taste buds, sense of smell ... ... infatuated with, drunk with!
It is strung out a good memory ... ...,
So spare time,
Gently read, slowly pondering ... .
the wind suddenly blew.

WONDERING
IN THE DREAMLAND
– The beauty
OF CHIANG KAI-SHEK
MEMORIAL PARK
中正紀念公園
園林之美

白千層
學名: *Melaleuca leucadendra* Linn.

樹幹呈褐白色，常會長出樹瘤，其淺褐白色的多層樹皮，是薄薄的木栓組織不斷向外增生所致，其質地疏鬆如海棉，小朋友常會剝取把玩或拿來當橡皮擦。葉子和相思樹類似，互生，全緣，葉與芽搓揉後有香氣，因含有芳香精油，可蒸餾做香料，亦可提煉白樹油。每年夏至秋季開花，花白色或淡黃色，頂生，穗狀花序緊密排列很像小瓶刷。蒴果杯狀，常仍附著在老枝條上。頂端成熟後3裂，種子細小。

Cajuput Tree
Scientific name: *Melaleuca leucadendra* Linn.

The barks are brownish white, often with lumps. The multiple layers of skin on its light brown white bark is the result of cork cambium. The tree skin is soft and spongy, thus children often peel off small pieces of the skin, with which they play or use as erasers. The leaves are similar to those of the Taiwan Acacia; they are arranged alternately, full-rimmed, and are fragrant when rubbed. Due to its fragrant essence, it can be distilled to make into perfume, or extracted to eucalyptus oil. Its flowers blossom in the end of the summer to autumn; the flowers are white or light yellow and are terminal, growing in closely packed spikes like tiny bottle brushes. Its fruits are cup-shaped capsules and to persist to old branches. When the tip is ripe it breaks into 3; it has tiny seeds.

香草植物

香草是指任何具有特殊香味的植物，包括根、莖、葉、花、果實、種子等，可供人類做為藥劑、食品、飲料、香水、沐浴或美容之用；我們常將它運用在美食的烹調，或沖泡成香草茶，製作成精油、香草醋、酒……。其中有些更具有殺菌、抗腐、治病的功效，還可帶給我們精神上的愉悅，放鬆緊繃的情緒，進而達到芳香治療的效果。
本區栽種的香草有迷迭香、薰衣草、茴香、紫蘇、九層塔、墨西哥鼠尾草、檸檬鞍、澳洲茶樹、香茅……等，其中也有臺灣原生香草植物，如馬蹄金、紅田烏、魚腥草、金錢薄荷、薄荷等。

Herb

Herb is a special flavor to any plants, including roots, stems, leaves, flowers, fruit, seeds, etc., for human as a pharmaceutical, food, beverages, perfumes, bath or beauty purposes; We often use it in food cooking, or brewed into a herbal tea, made into essential oils, herbs, vinegar, wine … …. Some more sterilization, corrosion, the effectiveness of treatment, but also bring us the joy of the spirit, relax your emotions, then aromatherapy treatment to achieve the effect. The area planted with rosemary, vanilla, lavender, fennel, basil, basil, Mexican sage, lemon saddle, Australian tea tree, lemongrass … … and so on, which is also a Taiwan native herbs, such as the horseshoe gold, red Tian Wu, Houttuynia, money mint, mint.

大卷尾
學名: *Dicrurus macrocercus*

俗名烏秋，嘴基有剛毛，全身呈現有光澤的黑色。尾羽相當長，末端外側明顯分叉。臺灣到處可見其蹤跡，包括城市、農村、平原、丘陵地帶與低海拔山區。常單獨活動，偶有群體覓食行為。多棲息於電線上，個性凶悍，尤其是繁殖期間，常會攻擊靠近巢區的動物，甚至人類，平常也會攻擊比牠體型大的大冠鷲猛禽。食物種類很多，主要以昆蟲為食，如蜻蜓、蝗蟲、虻、蠅等。鳴叫聲音為連續的粗糙『嘎啾-嘎啾-去嘎啾』聲，繁殖期間偶爾會有連續U型來回飛行的求偶展示行為。

Black Drongo
Scientific name: *Dicrurus macrocercus*

Also known as the king crow, it has beard hair and glossy black plumage. The tail feathers are very long and forked at the end. It can be seen everywhere in Taiwan, including the city, farms, plains, hills, and low altitude mountain areas. It is often alone, occasionally engaging in group foraging behavior. It often perches on power lines, and has an aggressive personality, especially during breeding periods, often attacking animals, even humans, that come near the nest area; it also attacks much larger birds. It eats many kinds of food, mostly insects such as dragonflies, locusts, horseflies, flies and so on. Its call is a continuous and rough "croak" sound, during breeding periods, it can occasionally be seen displaying courtship behavior—flying back and forth in U-shaped circles.

迷迭香
學名: *Rosmarinus officinalis* Linn.

迷迭香由於全株香氣濃烈，只要經過稍為碰觸，即可聞到它的香味，其用途廣泛，葉片可消除魚、肉類腥味，或加入煎烤、燉煮、醃漬於食物中增添料理風味，亦可用來泡茶、泡澡、釀酒、藥用、製造香料、提煉芳香精油，或製造香皂、乳液、乳霜、沐浴乳、洗髮精、香水等美容保養產品，是近年來極受歡迎的香草藥植物。依其植株外形和生長習性，一般可分為直立型及匍匐型二個品系。

Rosemary
Scientific name: *Rosmarinus officinalis* Linn.

With a strong aroma of the entire plant, one can simply touch a rosemary plant gently to smell its scent. With a wide range of applications, its leaf can be used to rid of the gamy smell in fish and meats, or be added to pan frying and stewing, or be used in marinate to enhance the cooking flavor of food. It can also be used in tea marking, bathing, alcohol making, medicinal use, producing seasoning, extracting fragrant essence, or for producing beauty care products, such as soaps, lotions, creams, bath gels, shampoos, colognes and so forth, making it a highly popular herbal, medicinal plant in recent years. By plant shape and growth habit, it can generally be divided into the upright and runner varieties.

澳洲茶樹
學名: *Melaleuca alternifolia* Cheel

如果稱它為互生葉白千層、茶香白千層、並葉白千層，就不會以為它怎麼跟我們所喝的茶不一樣，因為它和白千層是兄弟呢！從澳洲茶樹葉片萃取所得的精油具有治療、舒緩、殺菌和消毒的特性。目前市面上常可見到茶樹所製造的沐浴乳及洗髮乳等日常生活用品。您可以拿它和白千層比較看看，兩者是不是有幾分的相像呢？

Australia Tea Tree
Scientific name: *Melaleuca alternifolia* Cheel

To call it by alternate leaf melaleuca, tea-scented melaleuca, or symmetrical leaf melaleuca, it would not be strange to reckon that it resembles the tea we drink, for it is closely related to melaleuca. The essence extracted from the leaves of the Australian tea tree offers therapeutic, smoothing, disinfecting properties. There are household goods of bath gels, shampoos and the like made with the tea tree sold on the market. By comparing it to melaleuca, you will find a resemblance between the two.

香茅
學名: *Cymbopogon citratus* (DC.) Stapf.

屬多年生草本，具有檸檬香氣。臺灣地區在民國四十、五十年代，曾被大面積栽培，提煉香茅油出口，當時與薄荷油、樟腦油均曾為我國賺進不少的外匯。香茅草的應用極為廣泛，不僅可提煉香茅油作為驅除蚊蟲之用，亦曾被廣泛應用於香水、化妝品、飲料、香皂、清潔劑等之香精料。新鮮或乾燥後的檸檬香茅都具有宜人檸檬香味，可替代檸檬做為檸檬水用途。

Lemongrass
Scientific name: *Cymbopogon citratus* (DC.) Stapf.

A perennial herb, it contains a lemony scent. In the 50s and 60s, it had been brought in to Taiwan for large-scale cultivation extracting the citronella oil for export. Back then, peppermint oil and citronella oil earned Taiwan handsome foreign reserve. With a wide range of applications, the lemongrass is extracted for citronella as mosquito and insect repellent, and is also widely applied as fragrance base for making fragrance, cosmetic products, beverages, soaps, detergents and so forth. Emitting an enchanting lemony scent either fresh or dried, the lemongrass can also be used as an alternative to lemon water.

遊園尋夢
WONDERING
IN THE DREAMLAND
- THE BEAUTY
OF CHIANG KAI-SHEK
MEMORIAL PARK
中正紀念公園
園林之美

洪東標　花廊與樹影　38×55cm　2010　　Hung Tung-piao　Flower and Tree Shade

香草植物區，一座白色的花廊在小丘上彎出一道幽雅
的弧線，交錯的光影中和綠樹相映成趣。

In the Aromatic and Herbal Plants Garden, a white flower-gallery bends in an elegant arc, the crossing light and shadow
create an attractive sight with trees beside.

郭心漪　紅色寶石　38×56cm　2010　Kuo Hsin-i　Red Gem

香草植物區內的枸杞隨著微風輕晃，飽滿的果實在陽光的照射下顯得晶亮剔透，像極了珍貴的紅色寶石。

The Matrimony vine in the Aromatic and Herbal Plants Garden slightly swing with the breeze, the gorgeous fruits grow in plenty shine brightly in the sunlight, so much similar to precious red gem.

蘭花雨林區

蝴蝶蘭、石斛蘭……紛紛綻放花朵，
如彩蝶般在林間翩翩飛舞。

在杉木步道的引導下，進入了蘭花雨林區，
一叢叢嫩綠的山蘇花，如鳥巢般佈滿了榕樹林，
輻射狀地開展著寬大的線條，散發出熱帶雨林的氣息。

蝴蝶蘭、石斛蘭……紛紛綻放花朵，如彩蝶般在林間翩翩飛舞，
白、紅、黃、桃紅……為春天的綠布點綴繽紛的色彩！

夏天午后的小雨，不停地在池上畫圈圈，
而黑冠麻鷺快樂地一邊戲水、一邊覓食打牙祭！

水池旁，盛開的野薑花白如蝶，清香四溢，
貢德氏赤蛙「茍、茍、茍」……，低沉大聲的鳴唱著，
一同為雨林的夜，譜出仲夏奏鳴曲！

Orchid Rainforest Garden

Phalaenopsis, Dendrobium ... .blooming flowers such as butterfly-
like fluttering lightly in the forest.

Under the guidance of Chinese Fir trail, into the Orchid Rainforest Garden,
Patches of verdant fern, such as bird's nest full of tree-like forest,
Carried out a large radial lines, tropical rain forest atmosphere.

Phalaenopsis, Dendrobium ... ... have blooming flowers such as butterfly-like
fluttering dancing in the forest, White, red, yellow, pink ... ... for the spring the
colors green cloth decorated!

Summer afternoon rain, kept drawing circles in Ikegami,
The night heron and happy side of playing in the water while feeding sumptuous
meal!

Pool side, gray, such as ginger lily blooming butterflies, delicate fragrance,
Gunther's frog, "Gou Gou, Gou" ... . singing with loud low,
Night with the rain forest, compose sonatas summer!

遊園尋夢

WONDERING
IN THE DREAMLAND
– THE BEAUTY
OF CHIANG KAI-SHEK
MEMORIAL PARK
中正紀念公園
園林之美

蘭花

蘭科植物依其生長習性可分為地生、附生或腐生。萼片3片，花瓣3片，中央者為唇瓣，其主要功能在引誘昆蟲，達到授粉之目的。蘭科植物廣泛分布於全世界，尤以亞洲和南美洲的熱帶地區最多，喜愛常附生在熱帶雨林的植物中層枝幹上。一般常見的品種有嘉德麗雅蘭、蕙蘭、石斛蘭、文心蘭、拖鞋蘭、蝴蝶蘭與萬代蘭等。
台灣地處亞熱帶，多山多森林，所產的蘭科植物約有92數360餘種，為台灣維管束植物中種類最多的一科。蘭花是花中之王，養蘭、賞蘭已是現代人常見的休閒樂趣。

雨林

雨林大多數靠近赤道，雨量的充沛，讓植物生長快速，茂密的樹林孕育了成千上萬的生物，所以地球上有一半以上的動物和植物品種，都在雨林中出現。
雨林曾經覆蓋地球表面的14%，但如今卻只剩下6-8%；雨林被稱為「地球的肺」，因為地球大半的氧氣由雨林產生；也被稱為「世界最大藥廠」，因為大量自然藥物或藥物的原材料都在那兒找到。
熱帶雨林在台灣分布於嘉義到恆春半島，雨林植物的板根和氣生根都特別顯著。

Orchid

Orchid plants may be divided according to the growth habits of students, epiphytic or saprophytic. Sepals 3, petals 3, the central person for the labellum, its main function to lure insects to achieve pollination purposes.
Orchid plant is widely distributed in the world, especially in tropical regions of Asia and South America the most, like often epiphytic plants in the tropical rain forest on the middle branches. Common varieties of Cattleya generally, Cymbidium, Dendrobium, Oncidium orchids, slipper orchids, Phalaenopsis and Vanda so.
Taiwan is a subtropical mountainous Duosen Lin, produced by about 92 the number of orchid plants of more than 360 species of vascular plant species in Taiwan up to a Division. Orchid is a flower king, orchid, orchid tours is a common modern leisure fun.

Rainforest

Rainforest most close to the equator, rainfall is abundant, to plant fast-growing, dense woods gave birth to thousands of living creatures, so that more than half the planet animal and plant species occur in rainforest.
Rainforests once covered 14% of the Earth's surface, but now only the remaining 6-8%; rainforest known as the "Earth's lungs", because the Earth most of the oxygen produced by the rainforests; also known as "the world's largest pharmaceutical companies", because a lot of natural raw materials for drugs or drugs were found there.
Tropical rainforest located in Chiayi, Taiwan, Hengchun Peninsula, the board rainforest plants are particularly significant roots and aerial roots.

WONDERING
IN THE DREAMLAND
- THE BEAUTY
OF CHIANG KAI-SHEK
MEMORIAL PARK
中正紀念公園
園林之美

石斛蘭
學名: *Dendrobium phalaenopsis* Fitzg

石斛蘭是蘭科中的大族，擁有一千多種原生種，具各式各樣的植物體和花型。分佈在亞洲大部份的地區，是一種生性強健的附生性蘭花。由於花莖較長、花朵圓滿、色澤變化多，是切花及盆花的重要花卉之一。主要分布在中國、日本、東南亞、澳洲北部、新幾內亞等低海拔熱帶森林及太平洋的島嶼等地區，石斛蘭生長形式為附生於樹幹上或樹洞中，抗寒性性佳，是最耐寒的洋蘭。

Dendrobium
Scientific name: *Dendrobium phalaenopsis* Fitzg
The Dendrobium is an important part in the orchid family, containing over 1,000 of primitive species, of various plant corpus and flower form. The Dendrobium is an aerophyte with high surviving ability; it can be found in the most areas of Asia. With several characteristics as long scape, round and full flower, diversified colors, it is thus highly favored by cut flower and potted plant. It is mainly distributed in China, Japan, Southeast Asia, north Australia, and New Guinea as well as other tropical forests of low altitude and some islands in the Pacific Ocean. The growing method of Dendrobium is to attach on the trunk or in the tree cavity, with strong ability of cold resistance, it is the cattleya the most anti-cold.

石斛蘭

穗花山奈 (野薑花)

穗花山奈 (野薑花)
學名: *Hedychium coronar ium* Koenig

多年生草本，地下莖呈塊狀，且肥厚多肉，具有芳香。花序頂生，密穗狀，有大型的苞片保護，花白色，具有芳香，目前亦有育成彩色野薑花，有橘色、黃色等，每到夏天市場上常可見到販賣一束束芳香撲鼻的切花，它適合於水邊栽植觀賞，每年5~11月野薑花清香的白色花朵，幽幽的在水邊，山澗間開花，彷彿蝴蝶翩翩的飛舞在山巔，所以又稱蝴蝶花、蝴蝶薑、白蝴蝶花等。

Ginger Lily
Scientific name: *Hedychium coronarium* Koenig
It is a perennial plant; the stems underground are plump, robust, and fragrant tubers. The flowers are terminal, spike is dense, protected by large bud piece, and the color of this fragrant flower is white; while Ginger Lily of various new colors have been successfully cultivated, including orange and yellow; strings of perfumed cut flowers are frequently seen in market during summer time. This ornamental plant prefers growing along the water bank, from May to November, the fragrant and white Ginger Lilies quietly bloom in the gully and along the water bank, as if butterflies dancing around the hill summit, this is why its trivial names are butterfly flower, butterfly ginger, and white butterfly flower.

山蘇花

山蘇花
學名: *Asplenium spp.*

山蘇花或鳥巢蕨，是一般對鐵角蕨科巢蕨屬的通稱。這些蕨類植株都呈鳥巢狀，主要是為了適應高空著生環境，用以攔截從森林中掉落的水份及腐植質。臺灣共有三種，即南洋山蘇花、臺灣山蘇花和山蘇花。園區則有南洋山蘇花及臺灣山蘇花兩種。此三種的差異為：山蘇花其孢子囊長度約和側脈長度等長，且其株型較小，而南洋山蘇花和臺灣山蘇花株型較大，孢子囊長度約為側脈長度的一半。另外南洋山蘇花其葉軸在遠軸面具有顯著隆起的中稜，而臺灣山蘇花則無。

Bird's-nest Fern
Scientific name: *Asplenium spp.*
Bird's Nest Fern is the general name for Aspleniaceae-Neottopteris. The form of these ferns resembles very much to a nest, for better adapting to the conditions of high altitude, and for holding up the water and humus fell from the forest. There are three kinds of Birds' Nest Fern in Taiwan, namely Asplenium australasicum, Asplenium nidus L. and Asplenium antiquum Makino. The former two species are cultivated in this garden. The differences among them are: the length of Bird's Nest Fern sporangium is almost the same as that of lateral veins, but its plant form is relatively smaller, while Asplenium australasicum and Asplenium nidus L. are greater, the length of sporangium is only a half of the lateral veins. In addition, the midrib of abaxial surface is obviously higher at rachis of Asplenium australasicum, but not the case for Asplenium nidus L.

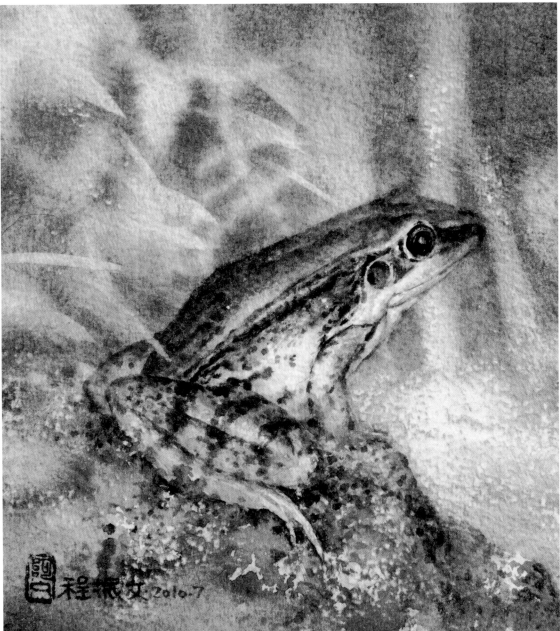

蝴蝶蘭
學名: *Phalaenopsis hybrida* Hort

蝴蝶蘭為蘭科植物中最具觀賞性的蘭花之一,因其花朵優美似蝴蝶而得名,在蘭花家族中有「蘭花之后」的美稱。蝴蝶蘭喜歡溫暖、潮濕且通風的環境,對光線的需求量高,但略低於嘉德利亞蘭、文心蘭、石斛蘭等。主要生長在暖熱的潮濕森林之中,在原生環境下著生於樹皮、樹冠、樹蕨及岩石上。一般栽培大多以水草為介質,極易栽培照顧。

Butterfly Orchid
Scientific name: *Phalaenopsis hybrida* Hort

The Butterfly Orchid is one of the Orchids with highest ornament function; it acquires the name for its elegance of butterfly shaped flower, and is honored as "queen of orchid" in the whole orchid family. The Butterfly Orchid prefers warm, moist, and ventilated environment, it also needs a lot of sunshine, but slightly lower than Cattleya, Oncidium, and Dendrobium. The warm and damp forest is the ideal environment for its growing, it can be attached to the bark, tree-crown, tree fern, and rock in the primeval surroundings. Generally, the waterweeds are mediums for cultivation; it is a plant very easy to plant and maintain.

貢德氏赤蛙
學名: *Rana guentheri* Boulenger

屬於中大型蛙類,有背側褶,背部棕色或淺褐色,嘴唇上下為白色,鼓膜周圍亦為白色,體側有不規則黑斑,腹部白色光滑。常可在平地和低海拔山區的水池、稻田和草澤出沒,平時不容易見到,繁殖期在水域出現。繁殖期為5月到8月,以夏天為主,生性隱密,叫聲很像狗叫,常「ㄍㄡˋ、ㄍㄡˋ、ㄍㄡˋ」的叫,而且白天晚上都會叫,生性害羞受驚擾時常會發出「吱」的叫聲,然後便跳下水逃逸無蹤。

Gunther's frog
Scientific name: *Rana guentheri* Boulenger

The Gunther's frog is of medium-big size, some folds are grown at its back side, the back is brown or light brown, the upper and lower lips are white, the area around tympanum is also white, both sides of its body have irregular black spots, and the white belly is quite smooth. They normally live in the ground and ponds, rice field, and grassy marsh in the mountain of low altitude, not easy to be seen at ordinary time, but will appear during breeding period. The breeding occasion for Guenther's Brown Frog is from May to August, especially during the summer time. The nature of this kind of frog is discreet, the sound frequently made by it, day and night, is very similar to bark of dog, "gou-gou-gou", and a sound of "zi..." can be heard when this shy creature is frightened, it would jump into the water and flee right away.

逐園尋夢

WONDERING
IN THE DREAMLAND
– THE BEAUTY
OF CHIANG KAI-SHEK
MEMORIAL PARK
中正紀念公園
園林之美

張明祺　蘭園
76×56cm　2010
和煦的陽光灑在琉璃瓦
上，襯托著樹影下優雅的
蘭花。

Chang Ming-chyi
The Orchid Garden
The balmy sunshine casts
its ray on the glass tiles,
accentuating the elegant
orchids under the tree
shadows.

李招治　哺育
75×55cm　2010

樟樹稍頂，枯枝橫陳，是黑
冠麻鷺的巢，天天等、日日
瞧，那自然探索的悸動，非
筆墨能形容。小黑冠麻鷺誕
生了，哺育的愛、生命的誕
生、成長的喜悅，是創作的
原動力，但盼畫面中除了繪
畫語言，還盈滿了深深地親
愛。

Li Zhao-zhi
Nurture

At the top of camphor tree,
lying the dead branches,
it is actually the nest of
Malay Night Heron; with
this everyday expectation,
everyday anticipation, there's
no word to describe the
vibrations created by natural
exploration. The baby Malay
Night Heron was born; the
devotion to nurture, born of
new life, and joy of growth,
are all driving forces for
creation, nevertheless, apart
from the painting language
expressed in the picture,
the deep love is enormously
inspiring.

蕨類植物區

蕨妙的樂章，寧靜...遼闊....自在......

蕨　為這片榕樹林，鋪上輕柔的絨毯，
沿著卵石小徑，穿越綠色隧道，
只見無盡的羽狀綠葉，濃密交織，
我彷彿掉進　原始的世紀中。

蕨　走過數億年的歲月，
看破了紅塵，
褪盡花的鮮麗、果的甜美，
只留下綠葉的輕快，
然後，
退隱山林，怡然自得。

初吐的新芽，曲線曼妙，形如問號......？
似乎，
看著人間的忙忙碌碌、爭爭奪奪，百思不解？

蕨妙的樂章，
簡單無華，不斷地重覆、無限地蔓延......，
寧靜...遼闊....自在....

Pteridophyta Garden

The fern-sensational symphony of tranquility, expansiveness and lightheartedness

The fern plants lay a soft carpet for the banyan woods,
Trailing along the pebbly trails, cutting through the green canopy,
Where it seems like an endless feathery green leaves, dense and interwoven,
I have most gone back to the primeval age.

The fern plants, which have progressed over millennia of time,
Seen the rise and fall of the mortal world,
Shed its flowers, and savory fruits
Leaving only the brisk leaves,
And then
exiled into the mountains for that carefree ease.

The tender shoots are in a sensual curve, and shaped like a question mark,
As if
it is puzzled by why people are always hurrying and fighting.

The fern-sensation symphony,
Which is simple, repetitive, extending indefinitely,
Of tranquility, expansiveness and lightheartedness.

蕨類植物

4億年前，蕨類植物的祖先早已遍布在地球的陸地上；目前世界上的蕨類約有12,000 種，臺灣就有600多種，其中至少有55種為特有種，密度相當高；蕨類喜歡在遮陰至半遮陰的林下、或溪谷等潮濕環境中生長，是非常重要的水土保持之地被植物。

本園蕨類區位於愛國東路側大孝門入口後的左方，前約有89種蕨類，多數為台灣原生的種類，少數為園藝栽培種，種類如：筆筒樹、臺灣桫欏、觀音座蓮、海金沙、臺灣金狗毛蕨、鐵線蕨、半邊羽裂鳳尾蕨、骨碎補、伏石蕨、波士頓腎蕨...等。

蕨類依其生活習性分有地生、附生及水生，，它們不開花、不結果，而以孢子繁殖的維管束植物。孢子囊群位於葉背，孢子囊成熟時會開裂，散出許多孢子，在適當的環境下萌發成配子體，再藉由其上精、卵之結合，產生下一代的孢子體。無論孢子體或配子體均可獨立生存，這是其他植物所沒有的特性。

Ferns

400 million years ago, the ancestors of ferns already all over the land in the Earth; the world are about 12,000 species of ferns, there are more than 600 kinds of Taiwan, of which at least 55 species are endemic, high density; fern class like the shade to half shade of the forest, valleys and other wet conditions or growth, soil and water conservation is very important to ground vegetation.

The Pteridophyta Garden located left side behind the Great Piety Gate, the former about 89 different species of ferns, mostly of native species, a small number of cultivars for the garden, species such as: Common Tree Fern, Taiwan Cyatheaceae, Vessel Fern, Japanese Climbing Fern, Taiwanense Cibotium, Maidenhair, Semi-pinnated Brake, Fortune's Drynaria, Little-leaf Lemmaphyllum, Boston Fern...etc..

Fern divided according to their terrestrial habits, epiphytic and aquatic, they do not flower, not the results, but with spores of vascular plants. Sori located abaxially, sporangia mature cracking when, shed many spores to germinate in an appropriate environment into gametophytes, and then on through the sperm and the egg combine to produce next generation sporophyte. Both sporophyte or gametophyte can be viable, this is not characteristic of other plant

筆筒樹
學名: *Cyathea lepifera* (Hook.) Copel.
北部郊山常可見到一株株宛如巨傘的植物，在步道旁為遊客擋住熾熱的烈日，這就是筆筒樹，莖幹上有葉片脫落後所遺留的葉痕，看起來像蟒蛇的皮，因此有「蛇木」的別名。經常成片生長在潮濕又向陽的坡面上，為了強化缺少形成層的莖幹而演化出的氣生根，它就是我們種植蘭花所需「蛇木屑」。有助於使它能牢牢抓住土壤，而能不斷的向上生長。

Common Tree Fern
Scientific name: *Cyathea lepifera* (Hook.) Copel.
In the mountain of north suburban area, numerous tall plants in a form of a huge umbrella can be easily seen; they are actually Common Tree fern. In a blazing sunshine day, they offer tourist a shady and cool place beside the trail. The trace left by fallen leaves on the stem, very similar to the skin of boa, is the origin of its alias - snake tree. They normally grow in clusters on the damp mountain slope facing sun, in order to enhance the aerial roots evolving from stems lacking cambium, it is the "snake sawdust" required for orchid cultivation; the aerial roots help the tree to hold firmly the soil and sustain its continuous growing.

腎蕨
學名: *Nephrolepis auriculata* (L.) Trimen
一般常以腎蕨的葉子拿來作為插花的材料，因為它很容易取得，又很有特色。臺灣原生的腎蕨科共有腎蕨、毛葉腎蕨及長葉腎蕨三種。常見的腎蕨擁有三種型態的莖，短直立莖使其葉片叢生；匍匐莖助其拓展族群領域；圓球形的塊莖則有儲存水份以備乾旱之需的功能。園區內另有一種長葉腎蕨，是原生的三種腎蕨中，葉片最大型的羽片，有短柄，不具耳狀突起。

Sword Fern
Scientific name: *Nephrolepis auriculata* (L.) Trimen
The leaves of Sword fern are commonly used as materials in ikebana, for its unique style and easy accessibility. The primitive species of Nephrolepidaceae in Taiwan include Sword fern, Rough Sword fern (Nephrolepis hirsutula) and Giant Sword fern (Nephrolepis biserrata). In terms of stem, there are normally three types, the short and straight stems help the dense grow of leaves, the creeping stems facilitate its family and territory expansion, while the stem tuber preserve water for emergent needs. There is another species of Giant Sword fern in the garden, its pinnate leaf has short stem but without ear shaped protuberance, and its size is the biggest among these three primitive Sword ferns.

鹿角蕨
學名: *Platycerium bifurcatum* Cav. C. *Chr*
具有二種型式之葉片，分為不稔性假葉呈圓形或扇形，原為灰綠色隨生長漸變乾褐色，能包覆基部之附著物，另一種為葉片為有稔性，葉背能生長孢子囊群，懸垂性，形似鹿角，全葉披覆一層柔毛。根基部位短而肥厚，基部可見黑褐色的鱗片，是附著他物生長的部位。栽培繁殖：自然情況下，鹿角蕨多附生於樹幹上，可自營生活。園區有兩種，即鹿角蕨及長葉鹿角蕨。

Stag's horn fern
Scientific name: *Platycerium bifurcatum* Cav. C. *Chr*
This kind of fern has two different types of leaf: one of them is round or fan-shaped phyllode of sterility, it is originally gray green but gradually become dry brown; it can cover the adherent objects; the other type is of fertility, some sporangium groups grown on the back of leaf, with suspending ability, the form is similar to a deerhorn, a layer of fine hair cover the entire leaf. The stem is short and plump, some flakes can be seen at the base, and it is the place to attach on the other objects for growing. The cultivation and reproduction: the Staghorn fern normally attaches on the trunk and is able to self-living. There are two types of fern in the garden, namely Staghorn fern and long-leaf Staghorn fern.

黑眶蟾蜍
學名: *Bufo melanosticus* Schneider
其體型大，由吻端沿著眼鼻線，經眼眶間達鼓膜上緣有一明顯的黑眶，因此叫黑眶蟾蜍，眼後有一明顯毒腺。體色會隨著環境而變化，常見為暗黃褐色，有深色斑紋，腹面黃色或淺灰色。無背側褶，前肢末端膨大。身體外表粗糙，佈滿大大小小的黑色腺性顆粒狀突起，和其極相像的盤谷蟾蜍的區別在於盤谷蟾蜍頭部背面無隆起稜。繁殖期約在春、夏兩季，卵產於深水坑。食物以昆蟲、穀粒、軟體動物為主。在低海拔的草地、空地間常可見到其蹤跡。

Spectacled toad
Scientific name: *Bufo melanosticus* Schneider
With a larger built, and a prominent black frame from its mouth along the nose line passing through the eye sockets to the drums, it is thus called the black-eyed bullfrog, which has a prominent poison gland behind the eyes. Changing its body color with the environment, it is often seen in a dark yellowish brown color with black spots, with a belly in yellow or light gray color. No pleads on the back, the toes on its front limbs are expanded. With a coarse body surface dotted with black glandular protrusions of varied sizes, it resembles closely to Bufo bankorensis with the only distinction lies in that Bugo bankorensis does not have the bump on the back. Its mating seasons are roughly in the spring and summer, as it lays eggs in deep water pits. It primarily feeds on insects, grain, and molluscas. It is often spotted in low altitude grasslands and empty spaces.

WONDERING
IN THE DREAMLAND
- THE BEAUTY
OF CHIANG KAI-SHEK
MEMORIAL PARK
中正紀念公園
園林之美

吳冠德　雨后新綠　39×54cm　2010

園區蕨類植物區茂盛的植物，充滿遠始森林的氣息，讓人很難想像自己身在台北市區，作者以輕快的筆觸，將雨后空氣中帶著濕氣，蕨類受光、反光與透光的美感表現出來。

Wu Guan-de　Fresh Green after Rain

The abundant plants in Pteridophyta garden are always filled with a exclusive sense of primitive forest, one could mistakenly thought in another place than Taipei urban are. With light writing style, the author presents the air with humidity, the beauty of ferns under the sunlight, light reflecting, and how they are pervious to the sun.

范植正　幽徑　76×56 cm　2010

中正紀念堂內，沿著大孝門側邊的卵石步道前行，即可看
到環境清幽的蕨類植物區，在濃蔭下營造出熱帶叢林的環
境，並栽植種類豐富的蕨類植物，彷彿置身於原始的山林
中，讓我們在都市中也可以享受一下原野的滋味。

Fan Chi-cheng　Serene Path

While walking along the pebble trail at side of the Great Piety Gate in the National Chiang Kai-shek Memorial Hall,
you may notice some extravagantly beautiful ferns are planted in a serene corner, creating a milieu of tropic jungle
under the deep shade. The visitors would even mistakenly think they are in primitive woods with these magnificent
ferns of so many species. People living in the bustling city may enjoy the natural beauty for a precious moment.

WONDERING
IN THE DREAMLAND
– THE BEAUTY
OF CHIANG KAI-SHEK
MEMORIAL PARK
中正紀念公園
園林之美

王瀚賢　綠光祕境　51×76cm　2010　　Wang Han-shien　The Mysterious Realm of Green Light

陽光由上灑下，使週遭的蕨類葉片青翠透光，隱身於茂密樹蔭中的石頭也反射著耀眼的陽光，任由葉影在石上輕快的流轉，也流露出綠色林間遮蔭處迷人的氣息。

With the sunray casting down, it illuminates the surrounding ferns with an emerald translucent light, and even the rocks hidden in the lush trees also reflect the glaring sun, where the flickering of the leaf shadows also conveys an enchanting ambience in the shady spots of the green canopy.

范植正　攬翠　76×56cm　2010

中正紀念堂的蕨類植物區，培育了許多不同種類的蕨類植物，其中幾株山蘇植於小水池中，莖粗短而直立，新生的翠綠色葉片由地下莖長出呈放射狀，陽光透過層層葉片，翠綠晶瑩，綻放　燦爛的生命力，枯委的黃褐色葉片則住下垂，生命的榮枯，形成冷暖色調，美而唏噓。

Fan Chi-cheng　Green Appreciation

Various ferns of different species cultivated in the Pteridophyta Garden in the National Chiang Kai-shek Memorial Hall, a few Bird's-nest fern planted in the little pond, its stem is short but straight, the newborn green leaves grow in radioactive direction from the underground stem; the sunlight passing through layers of leaf shines with an emerald color, magnificent vitality glows again while the withered yellow-brown leaves droop, the striking contrast between life and death signifying sadness in beauty.

大孝門

由愛國東路進入大孝門，花圃裡新種了幾排樹，
有春天黃花盛開的黃花風鈴木，以及秋天開著串串淡紫紅花的水黃皮，
馬路左側是蕨類植物區、肯式南洋杉林、及松樹林，
右側是一片香氣迷人的桂花林、一群筆直高聳的蒲葵林，
以及花團錦簇的紫薇花叢。

而桂花林，特別叫人難忘，
它雖一身素雅，微小的花朵亦不省目，
但每當小花盛開，散步經過的遊客，無不為它駐足，
闔上眼，忘我地輕聞陣陣的芳香！
然後微笑、沉醉在淡雅的氣息中！

濃密的桂花樹下蚯蚓特別多，是黑冠麻鷺覓食的好去處，
牠常如雕像般一動也不動，專注地細察落葉下的動靜，
連我如此貼近地按下快門，都置之不理，
但就在那瞬間，牠已迅速地從土裡拉出了一條蚯蚓，
如此出神入化的覓食功力，真叫人驚嘆啊！

The Great Piety Gate

Upon entering the Great Piety Gate from Aiguo E. Road,
there are several rows of threes planted in the garden.
There is the Golden Trumpet Tree that blossoms with yellow bloom in the spring,
and there is the Pongamia that blooms with strings of purplish red flowers in the autumn,
and to the left of the road are the Pteridophyta Garden, Araucaria cunninghamii,
and the pine woods,
and to the right are an aromatic group of osmanthus trees, a group of Chinese fan palms,
and the blooming purple rose bushes.

And the osmanthus woods are especially unforgettable,
being that the plant has an understated elegance and the flowers are inconspicuous,
yet it never fails to draw visitors to stop whenever its small flowers bloom,
drawing in their aromatic fragrance as one closes his/her eyes,
smiling gently being intoxicated in the mild, elegant fragrance!

There is an abundance of earthworms under the osmanthus trees,
making it a good feeding ground for the Malay night heron,
which stands motionless like a statue focusing on the movements under the fallen leaves,
and pays no attention even when I press down the camera shutter in such close proximity.
Yet at the moment,
it quickly draws out an earthworm from the ground to demonstrate a bewildering feeding power!

桂花
學名: *Osmanthus fragrans* cv. tre
桂花為常綠闊葉喬木，葉革質對生，葉形及葉緣會因品
種而不同，葉形橢圓至橢圓狀披針形，葉緣有全緣或具
鋸齒；一般而言，狹長橢圓形，幼葉邊緣有鋸齒。正面葉
色濃綠，背面綠色。開花以秋季最盛，花簇生，3~5朵生
於葉腋（呈聚繖花序），花小數多，多著生於當年春梢，
2、3年生枝上亦有著生，花冠分裂至基，為乳白色，香氣
極濃，有淡淡芳香，甜味，可加入茶葉中或添加於食品
中，增添美味。

The Osmanthus
Scientific classification:*Osmanthus fragrans* cv. tre
An evergreen broadleaf tree, the osmanthus has its
leathery leaves grow in symmetry, with the leaf shape
and edges vary by species, in ovate to elliptic, with
full edge or serrated edge; as a whole, it is narrow and
in an oblong shape, with serrated edges. The front of
the leaf is in a dark green, and a lighter green on the
backside. In full bloom during the fall, the flowers are
clustered, with 3 to 5 flowers growing under the leaf (of
a corymb inflorescence), with large numbers of small
flowers, often attached to the current year's spring
shoots, and also found on 2 to 3 year branches; the
corolla splits to the base, in a cream color, with very
strong aroma. It has a subtle, savory fragrance, and can
be added in tea or food to enhance the flavor.

黑冠麻鷺
學名: *Gorsachius melanolophus*
眼前藍色，嘴喙、額、頭頂及冠羽為黑色，褐色的身體、背
部為銹紅色有黑色橫漣紋，胸腹部棕黃色帶有銹紅色縱
斑。雄鳥眼睛的周圍及喙基部為藍色，頭頂、枕部的羽毛
為延長的黑色飾羽；而雌鳥則沒有這些特徵。分佈於台灣
北、中、南部低海拔山區至山麓一帶，但是在北部的近郊
及都會公園內繁殖族群數量正在擴增中。園區常可見到於
樹林下層尋找蚯蚓、昆蟲為主食，繁殖期約為3月至9月，築
巢於雜木森林或竹林間高枝上。

Malay Night Heron
Scientific classification: *Gorsachius melanolophus*

It is characterized with a blue spot in front of the eye,
black on the peak, forehead, top of the neck and crown
feathers, a brown body, red and black lateral patterns
on a brick-red back, and brick-red lateral stripes on
brownish yellow chest and belly. The male has a blue
outline around the eye and the base of its peak, black
ornamental feathers around the top of the neck, and
the belly feathers, whereas the female does not have
these characteristics. Distributed in Taiwan's northern,
central and southern low elevation mountainous regions
to mountainous hills, the number of multiplying colonies
in suburbs and urban parks in the north is rising. It can be
spotted often foraging on earthworms under the woods,
as it feeds mainly on insects, with the mating season
spanning from March to September, it nests on high
branches of mixed forests or bamboo forests.

黃花風鈴木
學名: *Tabebuia chrysantha* (Jacq.) Nichols.
黃花風鈴木是巴西的國花，又名伊蓓樹、毛風鈴、黃金風鈴
木，掌狀複葉，小葉4-5片，倒卵形，紙質有疏鋸齒，全葉被褐
色細絨毛。春季約2~3月間開花，花冠漏斗形，頗似風鈴，花緣
皺摺，花色鮮黃；花季時開滿整樹的黃花，頗為美麗。隨著四
季而變換不同的外觀，春天葉片脫落搭配著漂亮的黃花；夏
天長出嫩芽伴隨著吊在枝椏上的莢果；秋天則枝葉茂盛一片
欣欣向榮的景象；冬天又呈現著枯枝落葉的淒涼之美，呈現
四季分明不同的美感。

Golden Trumpet Tree
Scientific classification: *Tabebuia chrysantha* (Jacq.)
Nichols.

The golden trumpet tree is Brazil's national flower, and is
also known as Tabebuia alba, wind chime, golden wind chime.
With palm-shaped compound leaves, of 4 to 5 small leaves,
in reserved ovate, a paper texture with serration, covered with
fine, soft hair over the entire leaf. It blooms in the spring,
around February and March, with a corolla shaped in a funnel,
akin to a wind chime, with pleats around the outer edge of
a flower, and the flower in bright yellow; during the flower
season, the tree is adorned with yellow flowers to offer
visual appeals. With its looks changing along the seasons,
it sheds leaves in the spring dressed with the pretty yellow
flowers; grows the tender shoots accompanying the swaying
pods in the summer; fashions a bushy leaf growth in a thriving
prosperity in the fall; and returns to the lone beauty deprived
of leaves, projecting an aesthetical look revolving around the
four seasons.

蒲葵
學名: *Livistona chinensis* (Jacq.) R. Br. Var.
subglobosa (Hassk.) Beccari
棕櫚科常綠喬木，於公園、校園內常可見到。樹幹筆直不
分枝，成株呈灰褐色，外表粗糙，莖上節與節間不明顯。單
葉叢生於莖頂端，扇形深裂；葉柄具刺，葉柄成三角形，邊
緣有鋸齒狀的刺；葉大且呈掌狀分裂，裂片為線形，葉端
有分裂，而裂開的地方成弧形下垂，以前常用來做成扇子
又稱做葵扇，過去常可見許多阿公、阿嬤坐在樹下乘涼，手
上搖動的黃色扇子，就是葵扇。

Chinese Fan Palm
Scientific classification: *Livistona chinensis* (Jacq.) R. Br.
Var. *subglobosa* (Hassk.) Beccari

An evergreen tree of the Arecaceae family, it can be
spotted often in parks and on school campuses. It has
a straight trunk without branches, and adult trees are in
a grayish brown color, with coarse surface, nodes on the
stem inconspicuous. Single leaves cluster at the topside
of a steam, split deep into a fan shape; the leaf stem has
thorns, and in a triangle, with serrated thorns flanking the
edges; the leaves are large and in a palm-shaped split, in a
linear manner, and where the leaf splits it dips in a curve.
It was used to produce fans before, thus also referred to
as the palm fan, and it was the palm fan seen in the hands
of grandmas and grandpas fanning themselves with a
yellowish fan lounging and cooling off under a tree.

WONDERING
IN THE DREAMLAND
– THE BEAUTY
OF CHANG KAI-SHEK
MEMORIAL PARK
中正紀念公園
園林之美

曾己議　桂花小徑

57×38cm　2010

蜿蜒的小徑不時傳來陣陣的桂花香，兩旁相異的樹種
及後方高聳的棕櫚交織豐富的植物面向也賦予畫面不
同的層次美感。在小徑的引領下不僅是視覺感動也是
嗅覺的享受。

Tseng Chi-yi

Osmanthus Flowers Path

The fragrant of osmanthus flower comes from the
winding path, the trees of different species standing
on both sides, the back is the tall palms, and the
frequently interlacing plant dimension presents also
a beauty of various layers. Following the guidance
of path is not only an impression of vision, but also a
delight of smell.

許德麗　晨影　56x76cm　2010

大孝門進園右邊，有一片桂花林，花開季節清香飄逸，樹林濃密頗有奇趣，林下幽深是黑冠麻鷺喜愛穿梭行走的地方，畫中兩隻麻鷺正於清晨踱步林下，平靜怡然的神韻令人心中也不免開朗了起來。

Hsu Te-li　Morning Shadow

After passing through the Great Piety Gate, at the right side of garden, many freshly scented and fragrant osmanthus flowers gorgeously blossom. The dense woods are full of amazing treasures; the hidden corner under the tree is the favored place frequented by Malay Night Heron. In the picture, two Malay Night Herons stroll in the forest, all the sorrow would be dissipated by this serene and harmonious charm.

WONDERING
IN THE DREAMLAND
- THE BEAUTY
OF CHIANG KAI-SHEK
MEMORIAL PARK
中正紀念公園
園林之美

李曉寧　小花紫薇　37×56cm　2009

來去匆匆中正紀念堂多次，難得放慢腳步好好欣賞四周的
景物，走在廣場中不過是一牆之隔的城市喧囂卻像是千里
之外，高聳的白色建築和令人望而怯步的階梯，油然而生
的肅敬之情，令人侷促而不安，還好有兩旁的小花紫薇，
露出淡淡的笑容，像鄰家女孩般的靦腆，小小聲的向遊客
問好，慧黠的為莊嚴的中正紀念堂綴上了些許的溫柔。

Lee Hsiao-ning　Common Crepe Myrtle

So many times did I visit the National Chiang Kai-shek Memorial Hall, but all in a hurry; finally, I had this chance to appreciate the surroundings leisurely. It seems that I was in a totally different world while walking in the square with only one enclosing wall isolating the urban noise. An indescribable sense of veneration arisen when I stepped on the intimidating stairs and entered the high white building... Luckily, my restless feeling lessened by the lovely Common Crep Myrtle with a light smile, as if the shy little girl next door softly greets the tourists, cleverly adding some gentleness to the solemn National Chiang Kai-shek Memorial Hall.

鄧詩展　杉

37.5×50cm　2010

林蔭茂密的南洋杉是目前市區中栽植最多、最廣的園區。在炎熱的酷夏中漫步其中仍覺清涼、身心放鬆。

Teng Shih-chan　Pine

The dense and abundant Pine is the most and generally cultivated in gardens located in urban area. Even in an extremely hot whether, the fleshing cool offered by its shade soothe people physically and mentally.

遊園尋夢

WONDERING
IN THE DREAMLAND
– THE BEAUTY
OF CHIANG KAI-SHEK
MEMORIAL PARK
中正紀念公園
園林之美

郭心漪　挺立　30cm×76cm　2010
一群高聳挺拔的蒲葵，靜靜的矗立在大孝門的入口處，
像是在迎接進入園區的人們。

Kuo Hsin-i　Erectly Standing
A group of tall Chinese fan palm serenely stands at the entrance of the Great Piety Gate, as if greeting with visitors entering the garden.

吳冠德　松與風　39×54cm　2010

松樹在風中昂然挺立，滄桑有力的枝幹交錯天際，展現風骨。

Wu Guan-de　Pine and Wind

The pine tree stands proudly in the wind, the gloomy but powerful branches interlace in the sky, vigorously show its courageous characters.

WONDERING
IN THE DREAMLAND
THE BEAUTY
OF CHIANG KAI-SHEK
MEMORIAL PARK
中正紀念公園

觀賞鳳梨區

鳳梨的閩南語名字叫「旺來」，有吉祥之意，
所以讓它的名氣一路長紅，深受台灣人喜愛。

觀賞鳳梨區位於杭州南路與愛國東路角門附近，
在高大的黑板樹前的一處空地，栽植種類近17種之多，
如彩虹鳳梨、小型鳳梨、、擎天鳳梨、紅鑽石鳳梨、
小擎天鳳梨、達摩鳳梨、阿丹鳳梨、如意鳳梨、
蜻蜓鳳梨、珊瑚鳳梨、繡球鳳梨、絨葉鳳梨、火炬鳳梨...等。

觀賞鳳梨為多年生常綠草本植物，其共同特點是：
根部極不發達，水分和營養吸收主要靠葉片，
喜溫暖溼潤氣候，
它是典型熱帶或亞熱帶植物，原產於熱帶美洲，
適宜觀果、觀葉或觀花；
有些觀賞鳳梨成熟時，果實香味濃郁，
果肉的香度、甜度並不輸食用鳳梨，
可惜纖維較粗，仍不適合食用。

達摩鳳梨 尖端具有美麗鮮紅的葉、
火炬鳳梨 紅葉上有黃花，猶如一把燃燒的火炬、
珊瑚鳳梨 一粒粒的小紅花，狀如珊瑚、
以及蜻蜓鳳梨 美麗的粉紅苞片中鑲嵌著淡紫花.......，
一種另類的植物色彩，在這兒熱情地展開，值得您來欣賞。

Bromeliaceae Garden

The pineapple, which is referred to as "Wong Lai" in Taiwanese,
bestows the meaning of good fortune, which sends its popularity to soar,
and is beloved by the Taiwanese.

The Bromeliaceae Garden is located at the corner gate of Hangzhou S. and Aiguo E. roads,
and as many as 17 species are planted in a vacant lot in front of the blackboard tree,
consisting of the rainbow, petite, Ching Tien, red diamond, small Ching Tien, dharma,
Adan, Ruyi, Aechmea egleriana, coral, satinball, felt leaf, torch and so forth.

The ornamental pineapples are herbaceous evergreen plants,
and some of the common traits they share are: inconspicuous roots,
the leaf serves to absorb moisture and nutrients,
and the plant thrives in a warm, temperate climate, of tropical or subtropical origin,
and was originated in tropical America.
It has ornamental value of its leaves, fruit and flowers,
and some of them emit a strong aroma when mature,
no less than the edible species, except of the more coarse fiber that makes them inedible.

The dharma pineapple comes with pretty, bright leaf at the top.
The torch pineapple comes with yellow flowers on the red leaf, akin to a burning torch.
The coral pineapple comes with strings of small red flowers, liken to a coral.
And there is the Aechmea egleriana adorned with pretty pink buds imbedded
with light purple flowers.
There is a different kind of plant color that blooms here and beckons for your appreciation.

黃擎天鳳梨
學名: *Guzmania lingulata* (L.) Mez. Cherry
擎天鳳梨原產於中南美洲熱帶和亞熱帶地區，多生長在樹上或林中，附生或地生。喜溫暖、潮濕而排水良好的環境，但中午過強陽光又需遮陰。葉片革質、長劍狀，其葉片基部抱合於矮短的莖部，呈輻射狀排列。常見的品種包括紅色，紫色片，黃色的，橘黃色苞片，園區有三種。擎天鳳梨代表喜慶旺旺來的意思，常被運用於過年過節盆栽盆景造景中。

Guzmania Lingulata
Scientific name: *Guzmania lingulata* (L.) Mez. Cherry
The guzmania lingulata is originated in Central and South America and subtropical areas, often thrives on trees, woods, as an epiphyte or on the ground. Thrives in warm, humid, well-trained habitats, but needs to be shaded from the scorching midday sun. Leaves are in a leathery texture, in a long sword shape, and the base of the leaf wraps around the short, stubby stem, in a radiating configuration. Some of the common species include the red, purple, yellow and orangey yellow calyxes. Three species are planted on the garden grounds. The scarlet star projects the significance of impending festivity and good fortune, and is often used in potted plant arrangements for festive occasions and the New Year.

蜻蜓鳳梨
學名: *Aechmea fasciata*
又名萼鳳梨或粉菠蘿鳳梨，屬於多年生草本植物，原產巴西。所見粉紅色的鳳梨頭其實是苞片，真正的花朵為淺藍色的小花。葉片軟革質帶狀，葉緣有鋸齒。葉片基部包成筒狀可儲水，這類型的鳳梨統稱積水型鳳梨。葉表分佈有銀白色斑馬條紋，實際上為銀色鱗片所組成，可藉以吸收空氣中水分。整個花序開完可維持2~3個月的觀賞期。

The Dragonfly Pineapple Tree
Scientific classification: *Aechmea fasciata*
Also known as calyx pineapple or Bromeliaceae pineapple, it is a herbaceous perennial, originated in Brazil. The pink pineapple head that we see is actually the bud cover, and the true flowers are the small, light blue flowers. The leaf has a soft leathery texture in an elongated shape, with serrated edge around the leaf. With base of the leaves forming a cylinder that can be used to store moisture, this type of pineapples is collectively referred to as the moisture-accumulating pineapples. The silvery white stripes on the leaf surface are actually made of silver scales, used to extract moisture from the air. The entire inflorescence blooms over a 2 to 3-month display period.

珊瑚鳳梨
學名: *Aechmea fulgens* Brongn.
原產地為巴西、圭亞那，為鳳梨科蜻蜓鳳梨屬的多年生草本。能適應各種光線、溫度或濕度，生命力強，莖基部抱合而成筒狀。葉片柔軟，先端略下垂，反卷；葉面淡綠色略被白粉，葉背暗紫色，葉緣有鋸齒。花期秋至初夏，花季觀賞期長達3~5個月。圓錐花序呈珊瑚狀，小花粒狀，花瓣青紫色，花苞艷麗持久。

Coralberry
Scientific name: *Aechmea fulgens* Brongn.
Originated in Brazil, Ghana, it is a herbaceous perennial of the Aechmea genius, and the Bromelioideae family. It is adaptable to all kinds of Light, temperature or humidity, and highly resilient, with the base of the stems wrapped in a cylindrical shape. The leaves are soft and supple, and dip slightly at the tip, curled back; the leaf surface is in light green with white powder, and the back of the leaf in a dark purple, with serrated edges around the leaf. The flowering season spans from the autumn to the early summer, affording a flower-watching season of as long as three to five months. The umbri inflorescence appears in a coral shape, with small granule flowers, which have bluish purple petals, and the flower buds are opulent and long lasting.

WONDERING
IN THE DREAMLAND
– THE BEAUTY
OF CHIANG KAI-SHEK
MEMORIAL PARK
中正紀念公園
園林之美

李招治　旺來芳華　36×75cm　2010

人稱鳳梨「旺來」，總是有那麼點吉祥味！中正紀念堂園區裡，蜻蜓鳳梨的粉紅色花朵娉婷壯碩，讓人眼睛一亮。那綠與紅，有深有淺，帶墨或帶粉，在色彩的幻化中釋放隱藏在天地間的節奏與韻律，只要有心，必能領略那份不著痕跡的，超越自然的美。

Li Zhao-zhi　Charismatic Youth of Pineapple

Pineapple is also called 'Wong-Lai', a local name signifying prosperity! In the garden of National Chiang Kai-shek Memorial Hall, the pink flowers of dragonfly pineapple gorgeously bloom, attracting all the attention of tourists. The green and red are in different shades, with light black and pastel pink, portraying tempo and rhythm hidden in the nature through fantastic colors, the delicate exquisiteness beyond the beauty of nature could be perceived by anyone looking for it.

張明祺　鳳梨花　56×76cm　2010
嬌豔的鳳梨花像是火炬般，在墨綠的葉間閃耀著艷橘色的光芒。

Chang Ming-chyi　The Pineapple Flowers
The sumptuous pineapple flowers are akin to flames, flicking with is orangey flow amid the dark green leaves.

遊園尋夢
WONDERING
IN THE DREAMLAND
OF BEAUTY
OF CHIANG KAI-SHEK
MEMORIAL PARK
中正紀念公園
花木之美

球根植物區

一支支的花球，沖上了天　浪漫地綻放鮮花煙火秀！

這兒靠近愛國東路與杭州南路的角門，
栽種了10幾種球根植物，
有白肋華冑蘭、紫嬌花、百子蓮、
火球花、鱉蟹蘭、鳶尾、君子蘭、孤挺花、薑荷花、
晚香玉、蔥蘭、鐵炮百合、韭蘭、美麗文殊蘭……。

它花姿美妙，總為生活帶來好心情，
路旁繁星點點的蔥蘭、
明豔大方形如喇叭的孤挺花、
慶賀過年、添增喜氣的水仙、風信子、
點綴春夏風情的紫色鳶尾、
以及嬌柔迷人、傳遞愛情濃意的百子蓮……。

平日的它，平凡無奇　葉如草，
將一身的熱情，放進了球根，深藏土中；
但，
每當　花季盛宴的邀約到來，
一支支的花球，沖上了天　浪漫地綻放鮮花煙火秀！
讓人為它驚呼、為它喝采！

Bulbs Garden

A branch of the flower ball,
rushed the day of blooming flowers and romantic fireworks!

Near the corner of Aiguo E. Road and Hangzhou S. Road,
a dozen or so of the bulbous plants have been planted,
consisting of Striped-leaved Amaryllis, Nodding Catchfly, African Lily,
Blood Flower, Spider Lily, Iris, Bush lily, Amaryllis, Curcuma,
Tuberose, Autumn Zephyrlily, Longflower Lily, Rosepink Zephyrlily, Poison bulb.

Its sensual shape invariable brings a good mood to one's life.
The roadside stars of Autumn Zephyrlily,
The bright, trumpet-shaped Amaryllis,
The holiday festivity boosters of the Narcissus and Hyacinyh,
The summer breeze swaying purple iris,
And the sensual, titillating and love-conveying African Lily...

At normal times, it is ordinary with leaves as the grass,
its passion is packed into the bulb, buried deep in the soil,
Yet,
When the blooming season arrives,
Stem after stem of the flower clusters bloom in a romantic fireworks show!
It draws bewilderment and exhilaration.

鳶尾
學名: *Neomarica gracilis* (Herb. ex Hook.) T. Sprag
目前園區所種植的多數為巴西鳶尾，屬多年生草本。葉片呈
兩列像扇子狀展開。花莖較葉片長，外形與葉片極相似，像
是葉片開花，甚為特殊。花被有6片，3片白色平展外翻，3片
藍紫色向內捲。花謝後雌蕊繼續成長，成熟後直接長成幼
苗，因重量的關係而下垂到地面，根長出後，就形成新的植
株。花期在春天。園區還有種植雙色非洲鳶尾及青龍鳶尾等
品種。

Iris
Scientific classification: *Neomarica gracilis* (Herb. ex
Hook.) T. Sprag
A majority of those planted on the garden grounds are the
Brazilian walking iris species, and a herbaceous perennial. The
leaf opens in a two-row fan configuration. The flower stems
are longer than the leaves, with an appearance resembling
to that of the leaf, as if flowering on top of a leaf, making it
unique. There are six flower sheaths, with three white ones
extending flat outward, and three bluish purple ones curling
inward. The carpel continues to grow after the flower has
wilted and develops directly into a seedling, which tends to
droop onto the ground due to its weight, and a new plant
is formed once the roots are grown. The flowering season
is in the spring. The garden grounds also contain a two-tone
African walking iris and the green walking iris species.

鳶尾

百子蓮
學名: *Agapanthus africanus* (L.) Hoffsgg.
百子蓮為石蒜科百子蓮屬多年生球根花卉，開花後因種子
眾多而得名。葉叢生，基生葉，披針形，深綠色，先端漸尖。
花序為聚繖花序，花著生於花莖頂端，花莖實心直立，花期
在夏、秋兩季，花色有白色及淡紫色兩種。因花數量多，花期
長，且為特殊的紫色，常被運用為插花材料。

African Lily
Scientific classification: *Agapanthus africanus* (L.) Hoffsgg.
African Lilies are flowering herbaceous perennials of the
agapanthaceae family, and are known for producing great
numbers of seeds after flowering. The leaves are in a cluster,
basal, curved and linear, in a dark green color, turning pointy
at the tip. The inflorescence is in a pseudo-umbi funnel
shaped, with flowers growing on the topside of the steam,
it has a solid, upright steam, and blooms in the summer and
autumn, in white and light purple. For its long flowering
period and in a unique purple shade, it is often used as floral
arranging material.

薑荷花
學名: *Curcuma alismatifolia*
原產於泰國北部及東北部，為薑科薑黃屬(或稱鬱金屬)的
多年生草本。地下莖球形，常會著生數個圓形儲藏根。花
色以桃粉色為主，花期約在6月初至10月中上旬，花期長。
因花姿柔美類似鬱金香，故有泰國鬱金香的別名。薑荷花
是優質的切花與盆花植物，亦可作為夏季花壇栽培使用。
冬季莖葉會枯死，地下莖仍存活度冬，等到來年春天又會
萌芽、開花。

Curcuma
Scientific classification: *Curcuma alismatifolia*
Originated in northern, northeastern Thailand, it is a
herbaceous perennial of the zingiberceae family (or
curcuma genius). Its rhizome is in a rootstock, and often
comes with several spherical storage roots. Its flowers are
primarily in a peachy pink color, and it blooms form early
June to early October, with an extended flowering period.
For its subtle flower resembling the tulip, it is known as
the Siam tulip. As an excellent cut flower and flowering
potted plant, it can also be used for planting summer
flowerbeds. Although its stem and leaves will wilt and die
in the winter, yet its bulbous roots will survive the winter
to sprout and bloom again in the next spring.

百子蓮

薑荷花

蟹蟹蘭
學名: *Hymenocallis speciosa* (L. f. ex Salisb.) Salisb.
俗稱蜘蛛百合，多年生草本，具地下莖，為粗大球狀鱗莖，
外被褐色薄片，像洋蔥，但鱗莖有毒，如果誤食鱗莖會引起
嘔吐、腹瀉、腹痛及頭痛等症狀。植株外觀則易與文殊蘭混
淆，但文殊蘭葉片較寬。夏季開花，花白色，開花時數量多而
密集，且潔白清純，具芳香，極受歡迎。花瓣細線形，花瓣基
部三分之一處有扇形副冠相連，像極了鴨腳上的蹼。

Spider Lily
Scientific classification: *Hymenocallis speciosa* (L. f. ex
Salisb.) salisb.
Commonly known as the spider lily, a herbaceous perennial,
it contains rootstocks, which are large bulbous rhizomes,
covered with thin, sheer sheaths, akin to an onion; however,
the scaly rootstocks are poisonous, which when ingested
by accident can trigger symptoms of voting, diarrhea,
stomachache, headaches. The appearance of the plant can
be easily confused with the wild ginger, if not for the fact
that the wild ginger is wider. It blooms in the summer, of
white flowers, which appear in a dense cluster that are white
and pure, with fragrance, and are very well liked. The flower
petals are in a thin linear, and at one third from the base of
the flower petals is a connecting fan-shaped corolla, akin to
a duck's webs.

蟹蟹蘭

WONDERING
IN THE DREAMLAND
─ THE BEAUTY
OF CHIANG KAI-SHEK
MEMORIAL PARK
中正紀念公園
遊園尋夢

天南星科植物區

天南星科植物區，位於愛國東路與杭州南路角門處，
此區共栽植了天南星科植物28種，其他觀賞植物23種。

天南星科植物是植物界的一大家族，
主要分佈於熱帶及亞熱帶地區，
全世界約有126屬2500種以上，
台灣則分佈有16屬37種及3 個變種，
其植物有白色乳汁,該乳汁具有刺激皮膚的毒性。

它的葉色濃郁常綠、葉形大方、曲線柔美、又容易照顧，
所以成為最大宗的「觀葉植物」，
如黃金葛、蔓綠絨、彩葉芋、姑婆芋......。

而造形美麗獨特的肉穗花序與佛燄苞，
也讓它成為受人喜愛的「觀花植物」，
如火鶴、海芋及白鶴芋......，開花的時間多以春夏為主。

中正紀念公園茂密的榕樹下，許多植物並不易生長，
而園方用心地種植了耐蔭性的天南星科植物，
讓這兒變得綠意盎然。

Araceae Garden

Araceae garden is located at the corner of Aiguo E. Road and Hangzhou S. Road,
where a total of 28 species of family Araceae have been planted,
in addition to 23 species of other ornamental plants.

The Araceae plants are a big family of the plant kingdom,
which are primarily distributed in the tropics and subtropics,
with over 126 genera and over 2,500 species around the world.
Taiwan is home to 16 genera, 37 species and 3 mutative species.
The plants produce a white sap, which contains toxicity and can irritate the sin.

Its leaves are bushy and evergreen, large in size of a sensual curvature, and are easy to care for,
putting the plants as the largest family of decorative leaf plants,
such as Centipede Tongavine, Philodendron,
Angls' Wings, Giant Taro and so on.

With the distinct fleshy spike inflorescence and a curved bract,
which have made them a popular ornamental bloom plant,
such as Flamingo flower, Zantedeschia, Peace lily and so on.

Under the Chiang Kai-shek Memorial Park's bushy banyan trees, few plants grow well,
yet the park management's dedication in planting the shade-resistant
Araceae plants have transformed the area with a touch of green.

姑婆芋

學名：*Alocasia macrorrhiza* (L.) Schott & Endl

在還沒有塑膠袋以前，姑婆芋的葉子是菜市場的魚販或肉販，用來包裝魚肉的材料。屬多年生直立性草本，根莖粗短，具環形葉痕。葉片粗大，濃綠富光澤，一般芋頭則呈粉綠色。如果把水灑在葉片上，會擴散開來的就是姑婆芋，若是水滴成顆粒狀，就是一般芋頭。春季開花，佛焰苞肉質，綠色，雌花在下，雄花在上。漿果球形，紅色。因長得很像芋頭，因此常會被誤食，塊莖、花序及汁液皆含有劇毒，以根莖毒性較大。

Giant Taro
Scientific classification: *Alcosia Macrorrhiza* (L.) Schott & Endl.

Before plastic bags were invented, the leaves of the giant taro were what fish and meat sellers in the conventional market used to wrap the ingredients of fish and meat. A perennial upright plant, it has short, stubby roots and stems, with circular leaf marks. It has large green, shiny leaves, while the taro has a pastel green color. To tell them apart, water drops tend to diffuse on giant taro leaves, whereas they form water balls on common taro leaves. Blossoming in the spring, the flame-shaped flower buds are fleshy in a green hue, with the pistillate flowers at the bottom and the staminate ones at the top. The succulent fruits are in a spherical shape, in a red color. For resembling the taro, it is often eaten by mistake, and as its rootstock, inflorescence and saps are highly poisonous, most noticeably of a higher toxicity on its roots and stems.

火鶴花

學名：*Anthurium scherzericanum* Schott

原產非洲南部和美洲熱帶地區為多年生草本植物。花朵鮮艷奪目，佛焰苞像一枝伸展的紅色的花，花的中心豎起一條彎彎的金黃色圓柱狀肉穗花序，是我們觀賞的部位。全株直立呈有莖，或無莖或有攀繞性莖等型態，具有氣生的鬚根，革質的單葉螺旋排列在短縮的莖上，而其所謂的「花」，事實上是由花梗、苞片及肉穗花序所組成。目前是很受歡迎的切花及盆花種類，花色以紅色、橙紅色系為主，粉紅色系次之，而以白色系最少。

Flamingo flower
Scientific classification: *Anthurium scherzericamm* Schott

Originated in the tropical areas of southern Africa and America, it is a herbaceous perennial plant. With bedazzling flowers, the bract resembles a stretching flower, and erecting from the center is a curvy cylindrical inflorescence in golden yellow, which is the part we see. The plant is upright, either with stem, without stem or with coiling steam, and has epiphytic roots, and the leathery single left aligned spirally on short stems. The so-called flower is actually made up of stem, calyx and fleshy inflorescence. It has become a popular cut flower and potted plant species, with bloom colors primarily in red and orangey red, trailed by the pink, and least in white.

紅帝王蔓綠絨

學名：*Philodendron spp.*

蔓綠絨的品種繁多，分直立性和蔓性兩大類。若莖、葉柄和新葉呈紅色，且植株較大型即為紅帝王蔓綠絨；如果葉柄、新葉為綠色，即為綠帝王蔓綠絨。蔓綠絨性喜高溫多濕具遮蔭的環境，屬多年生蔓性觀葉植物，是極佳的室內中大型盆栽，夏天宜放在室內或遮蔭處，冬天則可放置於具陽光處。但若溫度太低，容易受寒凍傷而導致腐爛，須多加注意。

The Red Imperial Philodendron
Scientific classification: *Philodendron spp.*

There is an infinite number of philodendron species, which can be divided into the two categories of upright and runner. The red imperial philodendron is characterized by a reddish hue on its stem, stalk and new leaves, with a larger plant size; a green imperial philodendron is characterized by a greenish hue in its stalk and new leaves. Thriving in warm, humid and shaded habitats, the philodendrons are perennial ornamental plants, and are ideal as indoor mid to large size potted plants, best to be placed in indoor shaded areas in summer months, and in sunny spots in winter months. When the mercury dips, caution for rotting as the plant is prone to frost injuries.

WONDERING
IN THE DREAMLAND
- THE BEAUTY
OF CHIANG KAI-SHEK
MEMORIAL PARK
中正紀念公園
園林之美

洪東標　冬陽下的綠園道　56×76cm　2010
園區東南角門是通往杭州南路、愛國東路口的要道，冬陽下紅大衣
的老者漫步在綠園中，藍瓦、白牆、綠蔭、紅衣交織出一曲色彩交
響曲。

Hung Tung-piao　Green Pathway under the Winter Sun
The door at southeast corner of the garden leads to Hangzhou S. Road and Aiguo E. Road; the old man
walking in the green garden under the winter sun, blue tile, white walls, green shade, and red clothes
create a colorful symphony.

謝明錩　姑婆芋　51×76cm　2010　Hsieh Ming-chang　The Giant taro

姑婆芋在台灣隨處可見，屬天南星科，性喜陰溼。生長條件好時，葉長可至一公尺，高可達三、五公尺。在過往的農業社會時期，姑婆芋葉片是包裹食物的最佳材料，也是人們臨時避雨的小傘。這幅畫取材於中正紀念堂的蕨類植物區，那兒陰涼隱蔽的環境使姑婆芋成長的特別茂盛，光線與微風從隙縫裡篩進來，姑婆芋輕輕搖曳，在光影閃動中往往留下美麗的姿態。

The Giant taro or the giant elephant ear, can be seen all around Taiwan, a member of Alocasia genus, thrives in shaded and humid settings. When in optimal growing conditions, its leave can extend up to one meter long, and reach three to five meters tall. In the agricultural society of the past, its leaves were an optimal material for wrapping food, and a makeshift umbrella for people to shield from the rain. The painting is taken from the Chiang Kai-shek Memorial Park's pteridophyta Garden, where the wild taros thrive in abundance in the cool, shady environment, and where the light and breezes that ass through the gaps bring the wild taros to sway gently, leaving an enchanted form in the flickering of light shadows.

遊園尋夢
WONDERING
IN THE DREAMLAND
~ THE BEAUTY
OF CHIANG KAI-SHEK
MEMORIAL PARK
中正紀念公園
美林之美

虎背生態教學區

為增加中正紀念公園的生物多樣性與生態景觀，提供民眾與中小學生教學、環境教育與休憩的場所，同時也提供動物覓食、棲息、繁殖的環境，特別於虎背區闢建「生態教學園區」。

園區內依植物的生長特性與屬性，區分為臺灣原生植物、果樹植物及花卉植物等區，臺灣原生植物乃配合國中小學自然學科及生物科教科書中常見的臺灣低海拔原生植物為主，按北、中、南不同緯度之自然分布方式配置種植；果樹則區分為常綠與落葉性；花卉則依其生長特性與屬性分區種植。為方便民眾與中小學生更容易接近與學習，除於植株旁設立解說牌外，並編印生態教學園區步道手冊及自導式摺頁簡介，提供遊客能更進一步認識園區內的植物，進而能更關懷本土的生態與環境。

Hubei Ecological Education District

Chiang Kai-shek Memorial Park to increase the biological diversity and ecological landscape,
providing the public with the primary and secondary education,
environmental education and recreation place, but also provide animals for feeding, shelter,
breeding environment, especially in the Tiger back area Building
"Hubei Ecological education District."

Park, according to plant growth characteristics and attributes,
divided into native plants, fruit trees plants and flowers and plants area,
native plants is in line with national school natural science and biology textbooks commonly
Taiwan, low-altitude native plants mainly by North,
Central and South latitude of the natural distribution of different configure planting;
fruit trees are divided into evergreen and deciduous; flowers according to their growth
characteristics and properties are planted partitions.
For the convenience of the public and more accessible primary
and secondary students with learning, in addition to setting up explanatory signs
on the plant side of things, and production of ecological education park
and self-guided trail manual folding profile, to provide further understanding of the park visitors
can plant and then to more local ecological and environmental care.

2010.9

喜鵲
學名: *Pica pica*
18世紀自中國大陸引進，已為本地歸化種。目前整個西部平原有穩定族群；東部地區由於山脈阻隔，至近年宜蘭才有少量族群，花東兩地則尚無確切記錄。聰明且極富侵略性的鳥類，與人類關係十分親近。活動於平原及開闊丘陵的農耕地帶。雜食性鳥類，多在地面覓食，以昆蟲、蟲卵、蜥蜴等為食，有時也吃果實及種子。對城市的適應力相當不錯，不論公園綠地或者範圍大空地，都可獲得食物來源，常發出「夾喀、夾喀」的聲音。

Magpie
scientific classification: *Pica Pica*
Brought in from Mainland China in the 18th century, it has been acclimatized as a local species. Currently there are stable colonies through the western plains; only small colonies are spotted in Ilan as isolated by the mountain ridges in the eastern area, while there are no precise records in the Hualien-Taitung area. A smart yet highly aggressive bird, it forms a close bond with humans. It thrives on plains and in cultivated hilly agricultural areas. An omnivorous bird, the magpies feed on the ground, primarily of insects, larvae, lizards and such, and sometimes fee on fruits and seeds. Highly adaptable to urban settings, it finds food sources on park green and larger vacant areas, and often emits a 'chak, chak' sound.

樹鵲
學名: *Dendrocitta* formosae
體色大致以黑、灰與褐色為主。在臺灣是非常普遍的留鳥，分布於平地至中低海拔的山區森林的中上層。為雜食性鳥種，以無脊椎動物、昆蟲、花蜜以及漿果等為主食。成小群於樹林上層活動、警覺性高，發出「嘎兒-葛哩哦」婉轉的沙啞喉音或「嘎、嘎、嘎-」之警戒連續音。由於鳴叫聲特異且嘹喨，是很容易循聲欣賞的鳥種。飛行時會呈波浪狀，速度緩慢，翼上的白斑與白色腰部清晰可見。

Gray Tree Pie
Scientific classification: *Dendrocitta* formosae
The plumage is mostly in black, gray or brown. It is a common nonmigratory bird in Taiwan, distributed in flatlands and between the mid and high levels of mid-level and low-lying mountainous regions. An omnivorous bird, it forages mainly on invertebrate animals, insects, nectar and succulent plans. Move around in groups at the upper tier of the woods, it is highly alert, and emits a "ga gar" subtle throaty sound or a "ga ga" continuous alarm sound. For its distinct and resonating call, it is a species easy to spot. Flying in a wavy pattern at a slow speed, the white spots on the wings and the white waist can be spotted.

台灣熊蟬
學名: *Cryptotympana holsti* Distant
為臺灣產的蟬類中體型最大的，體色為黑色，且布滿金橙色的細毛，翅膀透明但前半翅的翅脈為橙褐色；此外，成蟲在複眼之間，有3顆閃亮的小單眼。每年5、7月，是臺灣熊蟬展現嘹亮歌聲的時候，叫聲為「夏、夏、夏…」一直叫個不停，彷彿告訴大家，夏天已經到來的消息，特別是每年夏天考試時節，叫得讓人有點心煩氣燥的感覺。牠的一生大半時間多在充滿危機的地底下度過，常可於清晨見到牠爬到樹幹上羽化的景象。

Formosan Bear Cicada
Scientific classification: *Cryptotympana holsti* Distant
The largest species of cicada found in Taiwan, it has a black body, covered with fine golden orange hair, and transparent wings, where the first half of the wing veins is colored orangey brown; moreover, the belly of adult cicadas has three shiny single eyes. In May to July each year, the Formosan cicadas make their annual calls of 'xia, xia, xia', nonstop, as if telling everyone that the summer has arrived, particularly ominous with a sense of trepidation during the annual exam time in early July. It spends most of its life span below the ground surface, where dangers abound, but can be spotted occasionally flying up to three trunks digesting early in the morning.

程振文 2010

南洋杉步道

讓一幕幕的心靈畫面，渲染著一遍遍的翠綠！

南洋杉步道位於中正紀念堂後方，
由信義路與杭州南路角門，或愛國東路與杭州南路角門進入，
即可發現步道的入口；
步道與杭州南路平行，貫穿虎背生態區，
高聳筆直的大樹多是肯氏南洋杉，少部分為小葉南洋杉。

林木的濃郁茂密，阻擋水泥高牆的灰冷，
杉樹的沁涼綠蔭，拭去沉悶炎熱的酷夏，
一窺　五色鳥發亮的羽色、喜鵲黑白身影的穿梭，
聆聽　松鼠彼此的大聲呼喚、熊蟬成群的盡情鳴唱！

來這兒吧！穿越綠色長廊！
讓緩緩徐徐的步伐，忘卻匆匆忙忙的緊迫，
讓一幕幕的心靈畫面，
渲染著一遍遍輕鬆的翠綠，
一片片遼闊的天藍，
快樂的黃、熱情的紅、一絲絲寧靜的雲白……

Hoop Pine Walkway

Let the images of your soul be infused with shades of green!

The hoop pine walking tails are located behind
the Chiang Kai-shek Memorial Hall,
where the entrance is situated at the corner of Xinyi and Hangzhou South roads
or through the corner gate of Aiguo East and Hangzhou South roads;
the walking trials are parallel to Hangzhou South Road,
passing the Hubei Ecological Education District,
with the towering, straight trees mostly being Araucaria cunninghamii Sweet,
and a small number being the small-leaf hoop pines.

The dense and lush pines inhibit the gray and tall concrete walls,
and the cool,
shaded greens provided by the pine trees are poise to rid of the stifling,
scorching summer heat.
A casual glance, there are Muller's Barbets with the shiny plumage,
and there are the magpies flash their black and white plumage.
To listen, there are the squirrel calls, and groups of cicadas sing
in a cacophony of noisy calls.

Come visit here! Pass through the long, green corridor!
Forget the hurrying stress by slowing your pace here,
and let the images of your soul be infused with shades of emerald green,
and the expansive blue skies, where there is the merriment of yellow,
the passion of red, and traces of the tranquil white clouds.

五色鳥

學名: *Megalaima oorti*

全身共有五種羽色，綠、紅、黃、藍、黑，以翠綠色為主，嘴粗厚且短，上嘴略長於下嘴，嘴鬚發達。眼部有一道黑粗的眉，胸部有一紅斑。分布於中低海拔之森林中上層。全身翠綠色在森林綠葉叢中為相當良好的保護色。單獨或成群在樹上活動，鳴聲「咯咯咯...」連續而宏亮，重覆不斷，類似敲木魚的叫聲，因此有花和尚的稱呼。雜食性，常以果實為食，亦食昆蟲。在枯木或枯枝上打洞築巢，強而有力的嘴喙啄成圓形的出入口，巢築於其內。

Muller's Barbet

Scientific classification: *Megalaima oorti*

With a plumage containing five colors of green, red, yellow, blue and black, the black-browed barbet primarily has an emerald green plumage, and has a thick yet short beak, with the upper beak slightly longer than the lower one, with prominent whiskers. Thick black brows frame the eye, and there is a red spot on the chest. Distributed in the middle and upper layers of mid- and low-lying forests, its emerald green plumage provides a fine camouflage amid the forest green. Moving alone or as groups, it calls out a steady "gu, gu" sound, resembling the sound of a Buddhist drum, thus earning it the nickname of a "crowing monk". Omnivorous, it forages on fruit and also feeds on insects. Nesting by burrowing holes in dead wood or dead branches, it chisels a round entry hole with its powerful beak, and builds a nest within.

肯式南洋杉

學名: *Araucaria cunninghamii*

原產澳洲，樹幹筆直，樹皮灰褐色；側枝輪生，上部枝條向上揚，下部枝條則為水平伸展，葉短針型，硬且尖銳。樹皮有橫紋，葉為針刺狀，雌雄異株，毯果闊卵形，果鱗先端銳尖具闊翅。臺灣各地庭園、公園、學校常見栽植作為觀賞用。樹皮汰舊時呈橫向剝落，新樹皮有金屬光澤的古銅褐色。另一種小葉南洋杉，則是枝條呈水平開展，葉鑿形，全緣葉端漸尖。

The hoop pine

Scientific classification: *Araucaria cunninghamii*

Originated in Australia, it has a straight trunk, with a grayish brown bark, on which side branches are grown in rotation, with the tip of the branches turning upward, while the lower branches extending horizontally, of short needles that are hard and sharp. With barks containing horizontal patterns, and leaves appearing in a prickly needle shape, it is dioecious, and has ovate cones, and the tip of the fruit scales containing sharp, wide wings. It is one of the common ornamental trees seen around gardens, parks, and school grounds around Taiwan. Old parks peel off laterally in regeneration, and new barks appear to have a coopery brown hue with metallic sheen. A related short-needle hoop pine species is characterized with branches extending laterally, with needles in a chisel shape of full edges turning pointy at the tip.

WONDERING
IN THE DREAMLAND
- THE BEAUTY
OF CHIANG KAI-SHEK
MEMORIAL PARK
中正紀念公園
園林之美

洪東標　運動園地
38×55cm　2010
肯氏南洋杉在虎丘上圍起了綠林道，是許多慢跑者的天堂；每天清晨映著朝陽，慢跑者揚起微塵，揚起追求健康的信心。

Hung Tung-piao　Sports Corner

The tall Hoop Pines enclose a green trail in the Hubei Ecological Education District. a favorite choice for many joggers; a slight dust made by these joggers in the daybreak time every day with a strong will for better health.

范植正　花和尚　56×36 cm　2010

「五色鳥」正如其名，全身上下一共有五種顏色，因每年四到六月，幾乎隨處可聽見五色鳥發出類似敲木魚的「郭、郭、郭郭郭…」的求偶叫聲。因而得到「花和尚」的綽號。由於中正紀念堂園區用心栽種大片茂密的林木，成為台北市區主要的鳥類聚集的天堂，因此我們才有幸在此目睹這些毛色亮麗的精靈。

Fan Chi-cheng　Muller's Barbet

Exactly as its name "five colored-bird", five colors can be found on this magnificent bird. The sound made by it, "guo...guo..." for courtship during April to June of each year, very similar to wooden fish knocking, the name Muller's Barbet is therefore given. Thanks to the dense woods carefully cultivated by the National Chiang Kai-shek Memorial Park, the area becomes paradise for the gathering birds; we therefore have the chance today to appreciate these elves with splendid colors.

遊園尋夢

WONDERING
IN THE DREAMLAND
– THE BEAUTY
OF CHIANG KAI-SHEK
MEMORIAL PARK
中正紀念公園
園林之美

張明祺　遊憩

76×56cm　2010

高高的南洋杉樹夾著林蔭小徑，遊人在這綠色隧道中找到都市中難有的閒適。

Chang Ming-Chyi　Recreation

With the towering araucaria flanking the shaded
trails, visitors find a rare ease in the urban
setting under this green canopy.

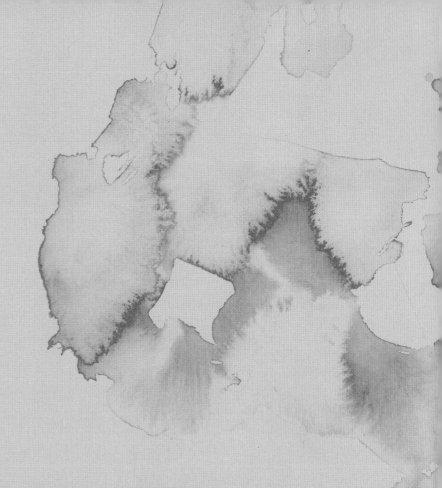

低海拔地原生植物區

是指台灣北部海拔500公尺以下，南部700公尺以下的地區，
是楠木類植物的天下，形成所謂的低海拔闊葉林帶，又稱樟楠林帶。
闊葉林對雨水有極強的截留能力，由於闊葉樹葉片寬闊濃密，
著生植物、藤本植物繁複，當大雨傾盆而降時，
雨水經過層層的截留，最後幾近滴水不漏，也不會直接打到泥土上；
所以闊葉林是水源涵養、保護土壤最有效率的森林型態。
可惜闊葉林帶屬較低海拔，也是人類活動最頻繁的地區，
人類的大量砍伐與人為造林，
讓大部分自然成熟的生態環境都已被破壞殆盡。

Low Elevation Native Plants

It refers to the region of over 500m above sea level in north Taiwan,
and up to 700m in south Taiwan, home to Laureceae plants,
which make up so-called low elevation broad-leaf forest zone,
or the camphorwood/phoebe forest zone.
The broad-leaf forecasts have a powerful rainwater retention capability,
and as the broad-leaf tress are characterized by a dense growth of broad leaves,
epiphytes and vine plants,
when the torrential rains pour down, the rainwater is filtrated through the layers,
catching every raindrop, and without hitting the dirt directly;
thus the broad-leaf forecasts are the most efficient forecast mode that nurtures
and protects the soil.
Unfortunately, with the broad-leaf zone being in the lower altitude,
where human activity is more frequent,
mankind's deforestation and artificial planting have besieged and destroyed a major
of natural, nature ecology environment.

原生植物

［原生植物］，是指原先自然生長於該地區的植物，土生土長的
植物，而非外來引進的植物，也未經人類因素移植。
［特有種］，是指因歷史、生態或生理因素等原因，造成該物種
的分佈僅侷限於某一特定的地理區域，且在其他地區並未出現
過。所以，台灣特有種植物也是台灣原生種植物。
原生植物是本土食物鏈的一環，它是本土生物的食草、蜜源、
食物體的重要來源、也是其主要棲息地；當外來種植物太多而
排擠掉本土植物時，將會造成本土性生物的食物缺乏，導致其
數量逐漸減少甚至滅亡。

Native Plants

The term "Native" plants refer to endemic plants that are
naturally grown in a region, rather than plants that have been
brought in, or transplanted artificially.
The term "specific species" refer to plants that are distributed
in a given geographical area due to historical, ecological or
other physiological reasons, and are not found in any other
regions. As such, Taiwan's specific species of plants are also
Taiwan's endemic plants.
As a link in the local foot chain, the endemic plants provides
an important source for the local living creatures that feed on
plants, nectar, and food substance, and a major habitat; when
an influx of foreign plants overtake the indigenous plants, it
will cause a food shortage to the endemic living organisms,
resulting in a dwindling number or even extinction.

WONDERING
IN THE DREAMLAND
- THE BEAUTY
OF CHIANG KAI-SHEK
MEMORIAL PARK
中正紀念公園
園林之美

北部低海拔地原生植物區

北部低海拔地區因受東北季風的影響，全年多雨潮濕，以殼抖科與樟科植物為主要樹種，如大葉楠、紅楠、樟樹、赤楊......等，林下植物有姑婆芋、野鴨椿、森氏紅淡比、蕨類......等。

東北部地區因受東北季風直接吹襲，葉子較小且厚、葉面有角質層、樹冠較圓且樹林也較低矮。

園區栽種有：厚葉石斑木、桃金孃、台灣金絲桃、烏來杜鵑、森氏紅淡比......等。

The northern, low elevation native plants area

As impacted by the northeast seasonal winds, the north low elevation region is characterized by a rainy and humid climate, and is home to plants of family fagacease and family Cinnamonum camphora, such as Large-leaved Nanmu, Red Nanmu, Camphor Tree, Red alder and so on.

The plants under the trees include the Giant Taro, Japanese euscaphis, Mori Cleyera, Pteridophyta and so on.

With smaller, ticker leaves, and collenchyma tissues on leaf surface, and of a rounder treetop and shorter woods, the specifies planted on the garden grounds include the thick-leaf grouper wood, Rhodomyrtus tomentosa, the Wulai azalea, Cleyera japonica Thunb. var. morii, and the like.

桃金孃

學名: *Rhodomyrtus tomentosa* (Ait.) Hassk.

桃金孃為原生植物，分布於中、北部低海拔山區，葉對生，橢圓形或倒卵形，厚革質，有三條顯著的直脈。花腋生，兩朵對生，花瓣5片，初開為桃紅色，將謝轉為粉紅色，雄蕊多數，花期春至夏季。果實呈壺狀，有宿存萼，未成熟時為綠色，初秋成熟，呈紅色或者紫黑色，成熟時果肉紅色，味甘，可食用。果肉味甜而有芳香，內含多數種子，可供生食，並製軟糖。

Rose Myrtle

Scientific classification: *Rhodomyrtus tomentosa* (Ait.) Hassk.

Rose Myrtle is an indigenous plant, distributed in low elevation mountainous areas in the central and northern regions, with opposite leaves in a oblong or reversed egg shape, of a thick leathery texture, with three prominent lateral veins. With flowers bloom under the leaves, they come in a pair of a five-petal shape, which bloom initially in a peachy red and slowly turn to a light pink, with stamen being the majority, blooming from the spring to the summer. With a kettle-shaped fruit, with calyx, the immature fruit appears in green, and ripens in the fall, in a red or dark purple color, and when ripened, the fruit flesh appears red, and is savory and edible. The fruit flesh is sweet and aromatic, containing a multiple number of seeds, which can be eaten fresh or made into soft candies.

台灣金桃

學名: *Hypericum formosanum* Maxim

常綠灌木，幼枝具四條縱稜，兩側扁平狀，成熟時呈圓柱形而具二縱稜。葉卵形或橢圓形，具腺體，明顯點狀。分布於臺灣北部，喜溫暖環境，生育適溫15~25度，栽培土以富含腐植質的砂壤土為佳。排水須良好，全日照，半日照均可。為台灣特有種，花鮮黃色很醒目，頗值得推廣種植，但由於原生地常會被割草割除或被其它植物演替，值得注意。

Hypericum Formosanum

Scienfic classification: *Hypericum formosanum* Maxim.

An evergreen shrub, its tender branch as four prominent lateral veins, with two sides being flatter, and appears in a cylindrical shape with two lateral vines in maturity. The leaves are ovate to elliptic, veins inconspicuous, with pale glandular dots. Found along Taiwan's northern area, it thrives in warm environment at an optimal temperature range of 15°C~25°C, best cultivated in sandy soil rich with compost. It needs good drainage and either a full day or half-day sunlight. An endemic species, it has prominent yellow blooms to call for widespread cultivation but needs to caution for being removed in mowing or being replaced by other species.

山黃梔

學名: *Gardenla Jasminoides* Ellis

屬常綠灌木或小喬木，葉子幾無柄，對生，橢圓形至倒卵狀披針形，先端漸尖，基部銳，兩面光滑無毛；具托葉。花白色，單一，頂生或腋生，子房下位，花香清雅，初開時呈白色，花將謝時漸轉為乳黃色。漿果，橢圓形，具5~8稜，宿存萼片冠狀，果實含黃色素稱為藏紅花素，因作黃色染料而得名「黃梔」，為古老的天然染料及食品的黃色著色劑，豆乾即以此為染料。

Gardenia

Scientific classification: *Gardenia jasminoides* Ellis

An evergreen hedge or shrub, the leaves almost have no stem, in opposite, or ovate or elliptic, tapering at the tip, with a sharp base, smooth and hairless on both sides; with leaf receptacle. The flower, in white of single flower, blooms at teh top or under the leaf, or below the ovary, with a gentle fragrance, which initially appears white and turns ecru as it wilts. Succulent fruit in ovate, with 5 to 8 edges, with calyx crown retained, and the fruits contain a yellow pigment called saffron, hence the name for the yellow dye, an ancient natural dye and a yellow food coloring dye, which is used to dye the bean curds.

中部低海拔地原生植物區

中部陽光充足、風害較低，以各種桑科榕屬、樟科楠木植物構成森林主要喬木。尤以台灣欒樹、台灣石楠、楓香......，在不同季節展現不同風華。
園區栽種有：木芙蓉、台灣欒樹、山黃梔、白花野牡丹......等。

The central low elevation native plants area

The central region has ample of sunlight, and lesser of the wind harm, is home to evergreens primarily consisted of family Moracease, Ficus genus, and camphorwood/phoebe woods. Particularly noticeable are Flame Goldrain Tree, Taiwan Photinia, Formosan sweet gum and so on that fashion a distinct flare in different seasons that fashion a distinct flare in different seasons.
Planted in the garden grounds include: Cotton Rose, Flame Goldrain Tree, Gardenia, white flower Melastoma and so on.

台灣欒樹
學名: *Koelreuteria henryi* Dummer
為臺灣特有種，屬落葉大喬木，樹皮褐色。二回羽狀複葉，小葉卵形，先端尖，有鋸齒緣。秋季開黃色花，頂生圓錐花序。果實為蒴果，由磚紅色的三瓣片合成，呈氣囊狀，成熟時轉為褐色；種子球形，黑褐色，有光澤。因葉形似苦楝故又稱「苦楝舅」或「苦苓舅」，因從整株綠葉到開花時呈黃色，結果時又轉為磚紅色，直至蒴果乾枯成為褐色而掉落，共有四色，所以被稱為四色樹。

Flame Goldrain Tree
Scientific classification: *Koelreuteria henryi* Dummer
An endemic species in Taiwan, it is a large, deciduous tree with a brown bark. Two layers of feather multiple leaves, small and ovate, sharp tip, with serrated edges. It blooms in the autumn in yellow flowers, with a top-growing cone inflorescence. Fruits are in a capsule, consisting of three brick-red petals in an air pouch shape, which turns grown when matured; the seeds are spherical, in brownish black, with luster. Also known as flamegold for its leave resembling a flamegold leaf, it is sometimes referred to as the four-color tree for how the leaves of an entire tree turn yellow when blooming and turn brick red when fruiting, and turn a dark brown when the capsule dries to fall off.

木芙蓉
學名: *Hibiscus mutabilis* L.
灌木或小喬木，單葉，互生，圓至心形，紙質，常5裂，裂片長三角形，先端長漸尖，圓齒緣，上下表面均佈滿星狀毛。花大，雌雄同株，腋生，花剛綻放時是白色或粉紅色，到了凋落前，則轉為紫紅色或粉紅色。蒴果近似球形，有剛毛，5瓣裂。另一種極相似的山芙蓉，葉片3~7裂，裂片扁三角形。花白色，變淡紅色。園區藥用植物區亦有種植山芙蓉，可比較它們的差別。

Cotton Rose
Scientific classification: *Hibiscus multabilis* L.
A shrub or small tree, it has single leaf, grown opposite, in a round to heart shape, often split in 5 of a triangle shape, with tip narrowing and a round serrated edge, with hair on the topside and bottom. With large flowers, it is monoecious, axillery, and first blooms to a white or pink color, and turns purple or pinky red before wilting. The capsule is near a spherical shape, with rigid hair, split into five petals. A species closely resembling the cotton rose has the leaf split in 3 to 7 places, with the fragments in a flat triangle. The flowers are in white and turn a light red. The Taiwan Cotton Roses are also planted in the park's herbal plant area, which can be used to compare their differences.

遊園尋夢
WONDERING
IN THE DREAMLAND
—THE BEAUTY
OF CHIANG KAI-SHEK
MEMORIAL PARK
中正紀念公園
園林之美

南部低海拔地原生植物區

南部嘉南平原一帶氣候乾、濕分明，冬季乾旱長達五個多月，因此植物利用落葉的方式來適應乾季，為南部低海拔原始林的生態特色。

南端恆春半島，熱帶海岸林極為發達，像是棋盤腳樹、欖仁樹、瓊崖海棠等，它們的果實會隨著海流漂流，靠岸後繁殖形成充滿熱帶氣息的海岸林。園區栽種有：海桐、珊瑚樹、相思樹、草海桐、棋盤腳樹、欖仁樹……等。

The southern low elevation native plants area

The south low elevation Jiayi-Tainan plains have an arid climate with distinct wet and dry seasons, where the winter dry season lasts as long as five months, thus plants shed leaves to adopt to the dry season as a characteristic in the south low elevation indigenous forests. On Hengtsuen peninsula at the southern tip, tropic coastal woods are prominent, such as Indian Barringtonia, Indian Almond, Indiapoon Beautyleaf and so on, where their fruits will drift with ocean current, land on the shore to grow into the tropical-ambience costal woods. Planted on the garden grounds include: Pittosporum tobira, Sweet Viburnum, Taiwan Acacia, Beach Naupaka, Indian Barringtonia, Indian Almond and so on.

穗花棋盤腳
學名: *Barringtonia racemosa* (L.) Blume ex DC.

常綠中喬木，葉互生，葉柄粗短，叢生枝梢，披針形或長卵形，先端漸銳，鈍鋸齒緣或波狀緣。夏季開花，總狀花序自枝頂下垂，花具短梗，白色或略帶淡紫色，是少數夜間開花的植物之一。核果長橢圓形，略作四稜狀，果實富含纖維質，可藉由水流來幫忙傳播。另一種棋盤腳，同為夜間開花，不同的是棋盤腳的花直立向上，而穗花棋盤腳是自然下垂。

Small-leaved Barringtonia
Scientific classification: *Barringtonia racemosa* (L.) Blume ex DC.

An evergreen tree, it has alternate leaves, short leaf stem, clustering, in ovate or elliptic, a slightly sharp tip, with jagged or wrapped edge. It blooms in the summer, and the cluster inflorescence dips from the tip of a branch, of a short flower stem in white or a tinge of light purple, and is one of the few plants that bloom at night. The drupe fruit is oblong in a slightly share shape, the fruit is rich with fiber, and the seeds are spread through water. Another species of Barringtonia racemosa also blooms at night with a distinction that it blooms upright, but the powder puff tree blooms dipping down.

穗花棋盤腳

海桐
學名: *Pittosporum tobira* Ait.

屬常綠喬木，枝條平滑，葉互生，簇生枝端，革質，倒披針形至倒卵形，中肋明顯。圓錐花序，頂生，黃白色，具芳香。蒴果球形，熟時呈橙色，開裂露出紅色種子。另有一種相近的臺灣海桐，為常綠小喬木，葉互生近於革質、長橢圓形，花序圓錐狀頂生，花朵甚小，但香氣很濃鬱，蒴果也是球形及橙色，又名「七里香」。下次碰到時可要仔細瞧瞧，不要搞混了！

Pittosporum
Scientific classification: *Pittosporum tobira* Ait.

A shrub or small tree, it has single leaf, grown opposite, clustered at the top, of a leathery texture, in reverse ovate or elliptic shape, and a prominent center vein. There has a funnel inflorescence, grown at the top, in yellowish white with aroma. The capsule is in a spherical shape and turns orange when matured, cracked to expose red seeds. A resembling pittosporum formosana species, an evergreen small tree, has alternate leaves of a leathery texture, in oblong shape, a funnel inflorescence grown on top with tiny flowers but with strong aroma and a capsule in sphere and in orange, also known as the Mandarin orange. Make sure you look close the next time and don't get them mixed up!

陳品華　海桐　38×56cm　2010

海桐是南部低海拔地原生植物。當花盛開時，遠看像米色
圓形的新娘捧花，一團一團的鑲在細長倒卵形長橢圓的樹
葉間，給人一種淡雅的美感。果實一顆顆小小圓圓的，全擠
在細枝頂端垂掛著，模樣叫人一看就喜歡。顏色由綠變黃再
轉成誘人的橙黃色調。整樹果實成熟時一串串黃橙橙的，
很像燦爛的小燈籠般掛滿一樹。我覺得海桐它多采多姿的
扮相可以和裝飾的聖誕樹比美了。

Chen Pin-hua　Pittosporum

Pittosporum is primitive plant growing in the southern area of low elevation. During the bloom season, the creamy, round flourishing flowers look like bridal bouguet in distance, inlaying in cluster among the long and inverted oval shaped leaves, creating an especially elegant beauty. The fruit of paulownia is small, granular, and round, packed in group, usually hanged at the top of thin branch, with a very adorable look. The color of flower would change from green to yellow, than turns into glamorous orange color; the matured fruits hanging on the tree, so much as bunches of dazzling yellow lanterns. In my viewpoint, the graceful beauty of Pittosporum is comparable to that of a perfectly decorated Christmas tree.

WONDERING
IN THE DREAMLAND
- THE BEAUTY
OF CHUANG KAI-SHEK
MEMORIAL PARK
中正紀念公園
之美

赤腹松鼠
學名: *Callosciurus erythraeu*

為台灣最常見的松鼠，身體背部毛呈灰褐色，腹部栗赤色。尾部毛長且膨鬆，在樹上跳躍時可借尾巴來平衡。自海拔3000公尺以下山區的闊葉林、竹叢都可看到牠們的蹤跡。屬雜食性，喜歡吃樹皮、樹葉、果實、花、芽及小蟲等，並且還有儲藏食物的習慣喔!吃東西時以前肢握住食物，送至嘴巴，尾巴還會翹起來，並且抖動，模樣十分可愛。叫聲如樹幹受風搖動而發出的「嘎嘎~嘎」的聲音。園區常可見到牠，但為了生態及不要影響牠們覓食的本能，請不要餵食牠們。

Red-Bellied Squirrel
Scientific classification: *Callosciurus erythraeu*
A common squirrel most often seen in Taiwan, it has a grayish brown color on its back and a reddish color on its belly. With a long and fluffy tail, it uses the tail for balancing leaping on the trees. They can be spotted in mountainous broad-leaf forests, bamboo growths up to 3000-meter altitude. Omnivorous, they feed on tree bark, leaves, fruit, flowers, buds and small insects, and have a habit of storing food! It is rather adorable as it feed with front limbs holding the food to the mouth and with the tails turned. Their calls resemble the sound of tree branches swaying along the wind. While it can be spotted often on the garden grounds, and to avoid impairing their feeding instinct and for safeguarding the ecology, please refrain from feeding them.

果樹植物區

台灣位處熱帶與亞熱帶地區，且海拔落差近4000公尺，造成不同的氣候帶，使得世界上許多果樹都可以在台灣生長，種類豐富又甜美，所以素有「水果王國」之美譽。

園區規畫果樹區，乃希望都市的孩子，
有機會目睹果樹的長相與習性，
也讓松鼠與鳥兒們，偶而可以加加菜、享受美食。
這兒種植了：香蕉、荔枝、、釋迦、柿子、芒果、
安石榴、金柑、柚子、楊桃、仙桃......等。

Fruit Tree Plant Area

Wth Taiwan situated in the tropics and subtropics,
with nearly 4000m drop in elevation from sea level,
it has different climate zones, and allow many fruit trees
around the world to grow in Taiwan,
producing a wide variety of succulent, savory fruits,
thus earning the fame of the "Kingdom of Fruit".
The plant now houses a fruit tree plant area, in anticipation
that urban children will have a chance to see what fruit trees look like
and their tendencies, and offer the squirrels and birds a chance to feed
and enjoy the treat. Planted on the garden grounds include the banana, litchi,
sugar apple, persimmon, mango, pomegranate, kumquat, grapefruit, star fruit,
caimito and so on.

白頭翁
學名: *Pycnonotus sinensis*

雌、雄羽色相同，全身大致為黃綠色，頭上至後頸黑色，頭頂白色，眼後有一圓形白色斑塊。在台灣西部平原至低海拔山區，是最常見的鳥種之一，多半棲息在市區公園、庭院、以及鄉間的樹林、農田、開墾地等環境中，多為人類經常活動之地帶。在人口稠密的都會區行道樹、公園綠地等環境，也可發現其的蹤影。鳴叫聲清脆嘹亮類似「巧克力、巧克力」。以植物果實為主食，偶爾會啄食昆蟲等小動物。

Chinese Bulbul
Scientific classification: *Pycnonotus sinensis*

Identical plumage for the male and female, it has a yellowish green plumage, with black on the head to the neck, and white on the top of the head, and a white circular spot behind the eye. A bird commonly seen in Taiwan's western plains to low elevation mountainous areas, its habitats include city parks, gardens and countryside woods, farmland, and excavated land, where people tend to congregate. It can also be spotted on sidewalk trees in densely populated urban areas and green parks. It has a crisp and resonating call, resembling "chocolate". It feeds mainly on plant fruit, and occasionally pecks on small insects.

安石榴
學名: *Punica granatum* Linn.

葉對生或簇生，長橢圓形。花腋生，花有單瓣及重瓣，重瓣花因花瓣多而呈彩球狀。花色有橙紅、粉黃或乳白等，以夏天最盛開。漿果球形，成熟時可食用。石榴據說是漢代張騫出使西域時，從安石國帶回來的，由於果實巨大如瘤，所以叫石榴。果實籽粒很多，古時拿來送給新婚夫婦，祝福他們「多子多孫」生生不息。石榴的花和果皮曬乾搗碎後，可拿來當作紅色染料，古時婦女就常用來染布做裙褲，皺褶的花瓣好似婦女的裙襬。

Pomegranate
Scientific classification: *Punica granatum* Linn.

The leaves are opposite or in a cluster, in an elongated shape. The flowers bloom under the leaves, and come in single and compound petals, with multiple-petal flowers resembling a ball-like configuration. The flowers come in shades of orangey red, pastel yellow or ecru, and are in full bloom in the summer. The succulent fruits are spherical, and are edible when ripened. The pomegranate was said to be brought back by Chang Chien of the Han dynasty from Kingdom of An Xi in his envoy journey to the West, and was named so for its enormous fruit. With many seeds contained in the fruit, it is often used to bequeath the newly weds, blessing them with posterity. Dried and meshed pomegranate flowers and fruit peel can be used as red dye, which women in the past used it to dye the fabric called pant-skirt, where the pleated petals resemble the edge of a woman's skirt.

香蕉
學名: *Musa sapientum* Linn.

為高大草本，莖短，埋在地面下，葉鞘肥厚互抱成假莖，葉叢出於假莖梢，有明顯羽狀平行脈，可摘取包束西用，亦常用來作粿的襯托。穗狀花序，分段開出，每段均有暗紫色苞片保護，苞片佛燄苞狀，披針形或卵狀披針形，開花後即脫落；花單性，花軸頂端向下彎曲，花束基部為雌花，上部為雄花，雄花早落。果實為漿果，肉質，長橢圓形，圓柱形或三稜形。

Banana
Scientific classification: *Musa sapientum* Linn.

A tall herbaceous plant, with short stem, which is buried underground, the leaf sheaths are thick and encircled into a false stem, from which the leaf clusters extend, with prominent paralleled vines, and can be used for wrapping, or as liner for the sticky rice paddies. A funnel shaped inflorescence that blooms in increments, where each increment is protected by a dark purple bud bract, which appears in a flame shape of ovate or elliptic, and falls off after flowering; imperfect flower, with flower tip bending downward, where the base of the flowers are pistillates and those on top are staminates, which fall off first. The fruits are succulent, fleshy, in ovate or elliptic, cylindrical or tetrahedral.

WONDERING
IN THE DREAMLAND
– THE BEAUTY
OF CHIANG KAI-SHEK
MEMORIAL PARK
園林之美

鄧詩展　蕉

37.5×50cm　2010

午後的虎背生態園區中，陽光透過杉木灑落
在蕉葉上。數片搖曳的透光，喚起在鄉間生
活的情趣，更有濃濃南國的台灣味。

Teng Shih-chan　Banana

In the Hubei Ecological Education District, the
sunlight sheds on the plantain leaves through
China fir. The swinging sunbeam passes pieces
of leaf, reminding the delight of rural life,
showing a strong taste of southern Taiwan.

周嘉成　松鼠　54.6×78.7cm　2010　Zhou Jia-cheng　Squirrel

松鼠在樹叢間自在的穿梭,動作既敏捷又迅速,敏感的牠,很難被鏡頭捕捉到,幸運的話,也許能碰上和他四目對望的情況。

The squirrel waves around the trees with ease, with swift and rapid motions. Its sensitivity has made it difficult to capture the squirrel by the lens, yet if you were lucky, you could catch a moment of staring into its eyes.

花卉植物區

位處虎背生態園區靠杭州南路的邊坡，
此區雖然狹長不大，卻栽種了豐富的花卉植物，
有仙丹、杜鵑、紫蝶花、麒麟花、文殊蘭、仙人掌、閉鞘薑……，
而且每種花卉都設立解說牌，
非常適合學子前來享受戶外生態教學。

Flowering Plants Area

Situated on the Hubei Ecological Education District near Zhanghou South Road,
a narrow area of modest size, it is however planted with an abundance
of flowering plants ,including ixora chinensis, rhododendron, blue butterfly,
crown of thorns euphorbia, poison bulb, cacti, crepe ginger and so on,where each
species of the flower has a description placard erected,
and is deal for students to on an outdoor ecological education.

樺斑蝶
學名: *Danaus chrysippus shrysippus* (Linnaeus)
樺斑蝶屬於中型的蝴蝶，前翅端部呈黑色，內有數個白色
斑點，故名「樺斑蝶」，本種幼蟲之寄主植物為蘿藦科之馬
利筋。雌蝶會將卵產於寄主植物的葉背，本種屬於多世代
的蝶種，意即全年皆可見到成蝶及幼蟲期，常可於馬利筋
附近同時見到樺斑蝶的成蝶及幼蟲。因馬利筋為有毒植
物，樺斑蝶較不怕鳥類等天敵侵犯，因此成蝶的飛行速度
緩慢，悠然於生態園中採食馬利筋的花蜜。

Plain Tiger Butterfly
Scientific classification: *Danaus chrysippus shrysippus*
(Linnaeus)
A mid-sized butterfly, the plain tiger has a black wing tip,
with several white spots in it, thus named the monarch;
milkweeds of the cancellata family are the host plants
for the larvae. The female butterfly lays her eggs on the
backside of the host plant's leaves, and the species if a
multi generation species, meaning that adult butterflies
and larvae can be seen all year round. It is often that
the plain tiger and its larvae can be seen around the
milkweeds. With milkweeds being poisonous, the plain
tigers are less fearful of their natural enemy such as birds,
thus adult butterflies tend to fly slower, feeding leisurely
on milkweed nectars.

萱草
學名: *Hemerocallis fulva* Linn.
又有中國人的「母親花」的別稱，俗名金針花、忘憂草、一
日百合等。葉自根部簇生，狹長呈劍狀線形。花莖自葉叢
抽出，頂部分叉，每枝著花數朵，雄蕊與雌蕊呈花瓣狀，每
日只開一朵，花期甚長。花形有單瓣或重瓣，漏斗狀，先端
淺裂或深裂，花色豐富。春至夏季開花，約3至10月左右。
可供食用、藥用、切花、盆栽、花壇和庭園露地栽培，主要
生產地在臺東大武、太麻里及花蓮的玉里等地，富有觀光
及產業價值。

Orange Daylily
Scientific classification: *Hemerocallis fulva* Linn.
Also known as the mother's flower among the Chinese,
it is called golden lily, roadside daylily or rail daylily.
Leaves grown from the roots in a slender, linear shape, and
flower steams extend from the leaf clusters, with a fork
at the topside and each contains several flowers, where
the stamen and pistil are in a petal shape, with one flower
blooms each day over a long period of time. Flowers come
in single and multiple petals in a funnel shape with

紫蝶花
學名: *Clerodendrum ugandense*
別名花蝴蝶、藍蝴蝶，為常綠性灌木，幼枝方形，綠色帶
紫暈，葉對生，倒卵形至倒披針形，先端銳或鈍圓，葉全
緣或有淺疏鋸齒狀。夏至秋季開花，圓錐花序，頂生，花
冠兩側對稱，花色為淺藍到紫色，花瓣完全平展，像極了
一隻展翅飛翔的藍色蝴蝶。杯形花萼5裂，裂片圓形，綠
帶紫色。有4條細長向前直出彎曲的花絲，為紫或白色。紫
蝶花可採用扦插法繁殖，生命力極強。

Blue Butterfly Flower
Scientific classification: *Clerodendrum ugandense*
Also known as the butterfly flower, blue butterfly, it
is an evergreen shrub with square tender branches in
green with purple tinge, leaves grown opposite in ovate
or elliptic, a sharp or dull tip, and slightly serrated edges
around the leaf. It blooms in the summer to the fall, of a
funnel inflorescence, grown at the top, with symmetrical
corollas on two sides, and a light blue to purple in color,
with flower petals fully flattened to resembling a flying
blue butterfly. The curved calyx split in five, of round
fragments in green with a purple tinge. There are four
filaments extending forward, in purpose or white. The
blush butterfly bush can be propagated through the
grafting method, as it is highly resilient.

樺斑蝶蛹

樺斑蝶

許德麗 紫蝶花
76×56cm　2010
花的形狀像蝴蝶，有美麗的藍紫色花瓣，原產於非洲，一年四季均會開花，又叫紫色精靈，栽植於虎背區.，記得要尋訪芳蹤，欣賞這些紫衣舞者在陽光下翩翩跳躍的美妙姿態。

Hsu Te-li
Blue Butterfly Flower
The shape of this flower is similar to a butterfly, with beautiful blue-purple petals; it's actually originated from Africa, blossoms around the whole year, "purple fairy" is its pet name. The flowers are cultivated in the "Hubei Ecological Education District"; do remember to pay a little visit and appreciate the graceful postures of these purple dancers under the sun.

逍風尋夢

WONDERING
IN THE DREAMLAND
THE BEAUTY
OF CHIANG KAI-SHEK
MEMORIAL PARK
園林之美

謝明錩　鳌蟹花　60×102cm　2008

螯蟹花又叫蜘蛛百合，在中正紀念堂的球根植物區，它是最特殊的植物。不開花的時候，螯蟹花看起來像看一株特大號的蘭花，開花的時候則像一群白色的長腿蜘蛛爬來爬去，既忙碌又騷動。從某些角度看它，又像兒童的風車玩具，一陣風吹來，興奮的彷彿要飛上天去。

Hsieh Ming-chang　Spider Lily

Amaryllidaceae, also known as the spider lily, is planted in the Chiang Kai-shek Memorial park's Bulbs Garden, where it stands out as a unique plant. Looking like a giant orchid when not in bloom, it is akin to a group of Long-legged white spiders crawling around when in bloom, appearing busy and moving. From certain angles, it is likened to the children's pinwheel toy, for how it appears to be soaring toward the sky when moved by a gusty wind.

謝明錕　杜鵑

51×76cm　　2010

杜鵑花在中正紀念堂應該算是最引人注目的花朵之一了，無論是靠近杭州南路的迴廊邊，信義路杭州南路交叉口的角門邊，或貯水區兩側的花圃，可以看到她們的蹤跡。杜鵑花是種類繁多的花卉，全世界有九百多種，台灣原生就有十五種之多，她主要分布在北半球的熱帶、亞熱帶與高山寒帶，中正紀念堂的杜鵑最常見的有白色、粉紅與桃紅三種色彩，三月時盛開，繽紛燦爛，煞是好看。

Hsieh Ming-chang
Rhododendron

The rhododendron may be considered as one of the most noticeable flowers in the National Chiang Kai-shek Memorial Hall. They can be easily found either near the corridor beside Hangchou S. Road, at the edge of corner door located in the intersection of Hsinyi Road and Hangchou S. Road, or in the garden at both sides of reservoir. There are numerous species of rhododendron, over 900 of them around the world, and the numbers of primitive species in Taiwan are as much as 15. They are mainly distributed in the tropic area, sub-tropic area of north semi-sphere and mountainous area in the Frigid Zone. The colors of rhododendron the most frequently seen in the National Chiang Kai-shek Memorial Hall are white, pink, and pinkish, the bloom season is March; the various colored flourishing flowers attract always the attention of visitors.

WONDERING
IN THE DREAMLAND
– THE BEAUTY
OF CHIANG KAI-SHEK
MEMORIAL PARK
中正紀念公園
美好之景

吳冠德　黃昏的杜鵑　45×38cm　2010　Wu Guan-dei - Rhododendron in the Nightfall
盛開的杜鵑在一場大雨後紛紛落下，在落日餘暉下引發　The blossoming rhododendron fall after a heavy rain, the endless gloominess can be sensed in the twilight at sunset.
繁華落盡的感慨。

許德麗　球薑
56×38cm　2010
虎背區有一叢球薑模樣很可愛，得彎下腰來才能見到橢圓形的球根花卉，花莖由地下抽出，花序橢圓卵形，透綠的顏色搭配一球球的造型很有特色，如果只站著走過便光看到它的綠葉而錯過了一次快樂的驚喜。

Hsu Te-li　Pinecone Ginger

Several lovely ball gingers can be found in the Hubei Ecological Education District, you have to bent for clearing viewing the oval-shaped flowers of bulbous roots; the scrape grows from underground, the bright green egg-like inflorescence go with ball shaped flowers is unique and exquisite; it would a pity to pass them by without paying a more careful observation.

盆景區．蘭花園

盆景區　緊鄰著杭州南路迴廊，目前此區尚未全時段對外開放，
僅於園藝技工進入工作時，方可進入參觀；
這兒是園區各類植物的後勤部隊，
一排排、一層層的植物盆栽，整整齊齊地排列著，
園藝技工正專注地整理、養護、培育、繁殖、分株……，
等它們健康茁壯後，再一盆盆移種到園區內的各處花園。

蘭花園　位在盆景區內，於96年底完成，
其以相思樹木柱搭設於金屬、PVC硬管結構上形成造型展示柱，
共有5支展示柱，將各種蘭花用水苔與竹片包覆後固定其上，
並有6座造型花床，其以鋼為結構，鋪設椰子纖維、水苔，
花床上架設定時噴霧系統，提供蘭花與周邊植物最適當的濕度與水分，
種植的蘭花包括香氣蘭花類、石斛蘭類及蝴蝶蘭…等，

區內設置一處生態池，種植了多種水生植物，
包含田蔥、睡蓮、水金英、人厭槐葉蘋…等，周邊並有傘草和白色野薑花；
螺類、水棲昆蟲、魚類、兩棲類，都已棲息其中，
這是一處觀察各種水域動植物生態的絕佳場所。

The Potted Plant Area, The Orchid Garden

The potted plant area,
located right next to the corridor by Hangzhou South Road, has not been opened to the public at all hours,
and it can be viewed by gaining the access when the horticulturalists enter the garden grounds.
It is the nursery for various plants in the gardens.
Row after row, and layer after layer of potted plants are lined up neatly.
The horticulturalists working diligently to sort, nurture, cultivate, procreate, splice ...,
And once they grow strong, the pots are then transplanted to flowerbeds around the garden grounds.

The orchid garden,
located in the potted plant area, was completed at the end of 2007,
Where acacia wooden posts are erected on a metal and PVC tube structure to form the display posts,
of five posts altogether, and a variety of orchids are attached onto them wrapped with moss and bamboo leaves,
along with six configured flowerbeds, which rest on a steel structure and lined with coconut fibers, moss,
and a timer misting system is mounted over the flowerbeds to provide moisture and water essential to the orchids and peripheral plants,
with the varieties of orchids including the fragrant orchid varieties, dendrobiums, cattleya species, among others.

There is an eco-pond in the area, which holds many aquatic plants, including philydrum, water lily, water poppy, floating moss, ginger lily;
Snails, aquatic insects, fish, and aquatic animals have taken refuse in it,
Making it a superb site to take in the ecology of various aquatic plants and animals.

蜻蜓

蜻蜓屬於蜻蛉目不均翅亞目，目前全世界約有三千種，臺灣已記錄的種類約有一百種左右。蜻蜓是不完全變態昆蟲，一生經歷卵、稚蟲、成蟲三個時期。蜻蜓為肉食性的昆蟲，飛行快速，會捕捉空中飛行的其他小昆蟲，大家一定聽過「蜻蜓點水」這句話，蜻蜓點水的目的其實就是在產卵，卵孵化後的蜻蜓稚蟲稱為「水薑」，水薑在水塘中則靠捕食水中的小昆蟲及小魚維生。

Dragonfly

The dragonfly is part of the infraorder Anisoptera, and has roughly 3,000 species around the world presently, with roughly 100 species documented in Taiwan. The dragonfly is an insect with incomplete morphology, as it goes through the three stages of egg, larva and adult insect. Dragonflies are carnivorous insects, and fly rapidly, and are capable of catching other small insects in midair. And as everyone must have heard the saying "the dragonfly touching the water", the purpose that a dragonfly touches the water surface has been to lay eggs, and the dragonfly hatchlings are called nymphs, which feed on small insects and small fish in water ponds

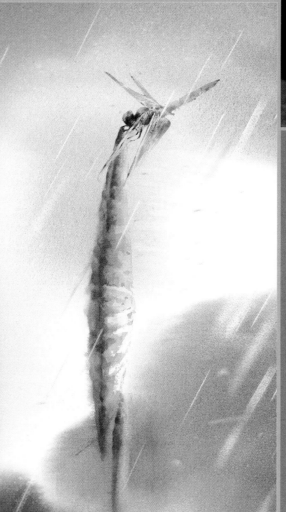

文心蘭
學名: *Oncidium flexuosum* Lodd.

文心蘭又叫跳舞蘭，因為其花朵很像跳舞的女郎，大多原產於熱帶美洲。屬複莖蘭，花色有純黃、洋紅、褐色花紋、斑點，開花季節不定，花期則長達1~2個月。又可分厚葉型、薄葉型，厚葉型生性較強健，生長習性與蝴蝶蘭相似；薄葉型性喜溫涼，較不耐高溫。栽植文心蘭要注意空氣濕度，不可太乾燥，材料可用蛇木屑、細石、木屑...等，但要注意保持排水通暢，繁殖方法以無菌播種、組織培養、分株法最常見，春天及秋天則是分株的最好時機。

Oncidium
Scientific classification: *Oncidium flexuosum* Lodd.

Also known as the dancing doll orchid, for how it resembles a dancing doll. Oncidium flexuosum is originated largely from the tropical America. A compound rootstock orchid, and blooms in pure yellow, orangey yellow with brown patterns and spots, its flowering season varies, but lasts for as long as one to two months. Divided into thick leaf and thin leaf types, the thick-leaf species is hardier by nature, and shares the growth nature remsembling to that of Phalaenopsis; the thin-leaf species thrives in cool temperatures and is less resistant to heat. A key in cultivating Oncidium flexuosum rests on monitoring the ambience humidity, as it cannot be too dry, and the materials include wood shavings, fine sand, snake wood and so forth, but cautioning for good drainage. It is propagated most often through clean seeding, tissue culturing, and dividing, and the spring and fall are a good time for dividing.

嘉德利亞蘭
學名: *Cattleya hybrida* Hort.

大多原產於熱帶中南美洲，它的品種繁多，花色變化萬千，花朵大姿態又美，有「蘭花之王」的美譽。嘉德利亞蘭生性十分強健，容易栽培，一般分成單葉種及雙葉種兩類，單葉種花期約在冬、春之間，花朵大，花瓣也較寬；雙葉種花期約在夏秋間，花朵較小，花瓣較窄，不過花色卻較為艷麗。嘉德利亞蘭生性耐乾燥，尤其近開花期需減少澆水，栽植地點需通風良好，陽台、大樹下均可栽植，若日照太強稍加遮光即可。

Cattleya
Scientific classification: *Cattleya hybrida* Hort.

Originated mostly in Central and South America, it has an infinite number of varieties and with great color variations, characterized by large flowers and sensual appeals, hence has been crowned as the "King of all orchids". Highly resilient, cattleyas are easy to cultivate, and are generally divided into the single leaf variety and double leaf variety, where the single-leaf species blooms between the winter and spring, with large flowers and broader petals as well; the double leaf species blooms between the summer and autumn, with smaller flowers and narrower petals, but in more brilliant colors. Cattleyas are draught-resistant by nature, and needs less watering when near the flowering period; the cultivation site needs to be well-ventilated, and balconies and spots under a large tree will do, simply by adding sunshade under strong sun exposure.

WONDERING
IN THE DREAMLAND
– THE BEAUTY
OF CHIANG KAI-SHEK
MEMORIAL PARK
中正紀念公園
園林之美

林玉葉　清香　76×56cm　2010
耀眼的光影下，花朵搖曳生姿，疏紅密綠的穿梭，美不勝
收，更可嗅到泥土的芳香。

Lin Yu-yeh　Pure Fragrance
Under the shadow of blazing light, the flowers gracefully dancing, between the beauty of flowers and leaves, even the fragrance of soil can be smelled.

劉淑美　蘭
55×39cm　2009
紫與黃綠在卡多利亞蘭間找到優雅的位置，
再次驚覺色彩自在悠游是如此美麗。

Liu Sue-mei　Orchid
Purple and yellow-green found their elegant
place in Cattleya orchid, surprisingly to
realize again, that the carefree journeying
color can be so gracefully beautiful.

WONDERING
IN THE DREAMLAND
－THE BEAUTY
OF CHIANG KAI-SHEK
MEMORIAL PARK
中正紀念公園
園林之美

藥用植物區

尋尋覓覓的…，不只是療癒身體的藥草，更是醫治心靈的良藥吧……！

本區位於信義路與杭州南路角門前方，
藥用植物泛指具有藥效成分，可以用來治病或對生物有益的植物，
藥用的部位可能是整株或其根、莖、葉、花、果實或種子，
植物是「人類的大藥廠」，大多藥物的材料都需取自於它們。

本區共篩選常用、實用且較具觀賞性之藥用植物40餘種，
如：益母草、土半夏、兔仔菜、燈籠草、白鶴靈芝、仙草、
明日葉、魚腥草、閉鞘薑、艾草、薄荷、青葙、枸杞……等。

沉默寡言的植物，永遠是人們的良醫，
第一帖良藥：愉悅清靜的空氣，
第二帖良藥：健康純淨的菜餚，
第三帖良藥：醫治百病的千花萬草，
第四帖良藥：……。

「松下問童子，言師採藥去，只在此山中，雲深不知處……」
也許，師父在深山中尋尋覓覓的…，
不只是療癒身體的藥草，
更是醫治心靈的良藥吧……！

Taiwan's Herb Garden

Looking high and low, .. it is beyond the herbs that heal the body but an elixir that heals the spirituality

With the area located in front of the corner gate between Xinyi Road and Hangzhou S. Road,
Medicinal plants broadly refer to plants that come with medicinal contents that are used for treating disease or are deemed biophysically beneficial.
The parts of the medicinal plants can come from the roots, stalks, leaves, flowers, fruits, or seeds.
Billed as the mankind's pharmacy, the ingredients of many medicines have derived from plants.

The area has selected over 40 species of the common, practical, appealing medicinal plants, such as Motherwort, Divaricate Typhonium, Chinese Ixeris, Cut-leaf Ground Berry, White crane flower, Mesona, Moringa Tree, Pig Thigh, Crepe Ginger, Artemisias, Peppermint, Feather Cockscomb, Matrimony vine and so on.

The silent plants provide a source of healing power to mankind,
Elixir one: the joyous, refreshing air.
Elixir two: the healthy and pure meal,
Elixir three: the many plants that heal all sorts of ills
Elixir four: and the list goes on

"Asking a child under the pine tree, who says my mentor has gone looking for herbs, somewhere deep in the mountain, where the clouds obscure …
Perhaps, what the mentor is looking for is more than the herbs that heal the body but an elixir that heals the spirituality!

魚腥草
學名: *Houttuynia cordata* Thunb.
屬於三白草科蕺菜屬，又名蕺菜，多年生草本，莖可分為地上直立莖及地下匍匐性兩部份，根莖的節處具有輪生狀的根，易於繁殖，心形葉片互生於直立莖上。花序頂生，起先由總苞片保護住，內部花朵發育成熟時，由4片苞片展開成雪白的花瓣狀，中間則露出由上百朵小花所構成的淡黃色穗狀花序。被碰觸後散發防禦性的魚腥臭味，自古即被中醫認定具有清熱解毒、祛痰止咳的功效，因含有魚腥草素，具有抗菌、抗病毒及增強免疫力的效果，是一種藥、食兼備的植物。

The chameleon
Scientific classification: *Houttuynia cordata* Thunb.
A member of the Saurauraceae family, it is also known as the chameleon; an annual herb, its stem consists of the upright stem above the ground and the runner stem below the ground, with circular roots around the node of the root stem, making it easy to propagate, and the heart-shaped leaves alternate on the upright stem. A topside inflorescence which is protected by two bracts initially, and when the flower matures within, four bracts open to a snow-white petal shape, and exposed from it is a light-yellow clustering inflorescence made up of hundreds of tiny flowers. Emits a defensive fishy odor when touched, and is regarded in Chinese medicine to offer cooing, detox, phlegm and cough healing property, and for containing diuretic, it offers antibacterial, anti-inflammatory, antiviral and immunity enhancing properties, a medicinal and edible plant.

紫蘇
學名: *Perilla frutescens* (L.) Britt.
屬一年生草本，全株呈紫色或紫綠色。葉對生，圓卵形，先端長尖，基部截形，鈍鋸齒緣。總狀花序，頂生或腋生。紫蘇葉紫而背白，和另一種葉綠背白的白蘇有別，入藥以紫蘇的效果較佳。紫蘇目前廣泛應用作香料及食品，例如葉花蒸餾精油可作為牙膏、清潔劑及化妝品等芳香原料，並具有殺菌性，做為醬油、醃漬物等之添加物如紫蘇梅、紫蘇脆瓜等。

Perilla
Scientific classification: *Perilla frutescens* (L.) Britt.
An annual herb, the plant appears in purple or purplish green. Leaves are grown opposite, ovate, with long tips at the end, with the base in a snap shape, and dull serration around. Has a cluster inflorescence, grown at the topside of under the leaf. The purpose perilla leaves are purple on top and white on the back, which differ from the white perilla, which ahs a green leave and white back, and the former often proper a better medicinal property. The perilla is widely used as aroma and food; for instance, the leaf/flower steamed extract is used for making toothpaste, detergent and as cosmetic fragrance, and has disinfecting property as an additive in soy sauce, marinate, such as perilla-flavored plus and pickles.

仙草
學名: *Mesona chinensis* Benth
一年生草本，莖上部直立，下部伏地，四方形，被長柔毛或細剛毛。葉對生，葉片狹卵形或寬卵圓形，先端急尖或鈍，基部寬楔形或圓，邊緣具鋸齒，兩面被細剛毛或柔毛。輪傘花序多花，組成總狀花序，頂生或生於側枝，花期7~10月。仙草茶是青草茶中很常用的一種，作法簡單，只要後將曬乾的仙草莖葉加水50倍以上，熬煮1~2小時過濾即可，其濾汁加入少量的澱粉就能變成大量的仙草凍。

The mesona
Scientific classification: *Mesona chinensis* Benth
A herbaceous annual, its stem appears upright on top, and hugs the ground at the bottom, in a square shape, covered with soft or rigid hair. Leaves grown opposite, in ovate or elliptic, with a sharp or dull tip and a base in a wide chisel or round shape with serrated edges, and coated with rigid or soft hair. The umbrella inflorescence of compound flowers assembles to a cluster inflorescence, grown on the topside or by lateral branches, and flowering in July to October. The mesona drink is a common herbal drink, which is easy to make, simply by adding 50 parts of water to dried mesona leaves and stems, cooking for 1 to 2 hours and filtrate the content, where adding a small amount of starch to the filtrated juice will turn to voluminous mesona jelly.

WONDERING
IN THE DREAMLAND
– THE BEAUTY
OF CHIANG KAI-SHEK
MEMORIAL PARK
中正紀念公園
園林之美

劉淑美　穿過-藥園　55×39cm　2010
園區內並不起眼的藥草，靜候偶至的遊客，而她僅僅慢慢穿過蜿蜒小路。園內榕樹壯碩，與遠處若直若曲的林木有著對比的趣味。

Liu Sue-mei　Pass through-Taiwan's Herb Garden
The unnoticeable medicinal herbs in the garden patiently wait for the occasionally visits of tourist, but she just passed slowly through the winding pathway. A contrast sight is created by the grand banyan and distant several straight or bent trees.

鄧詩展　迴廊
37.5×50cm　2010
圍繞整個園區的迴廊，在滿是綠意的
氛圍中，提供給每一位到訪的遊客尋
幽思古的情懷。

Teng Shih-chan　Corridor
The Corridor surrounding the entire
garden is in a all green atmosphere,
introducing a sense of finding secluded
place and yearning or the old times to
each visitor.

櫻花區

滿枝淡淡紅紅，春詩篇篇頁頁，
微風徐徐、花雨紛紛飛飛，
離別，緩些緩些……，
漫漫　飄飄　醉醉　歇歇，
夢醒
卻已　綠綠葉葉……。

Cherry Garden

A subtle shade of red adorning the branches;
the poetry of the spring embellishing the many poems,
As caressed by the gentle breeze, falling gently is the rain of cheery blossom petals.
Farewell, slowly, unhurriedly …
Floating, falling mesmerizing, rendering
Yet when awaken,
All that remain are the green leaves …

原生櫻花區

由堂體往信義路、杭州南路角門之透水步道兩側，即為中正紀念公園之原生櫻花區。櫻花在植物分類上屬於薔薇科、梅屬，梅屬全世界約有200種，主要分布在北半球的溫帶地區，臺灣大約有10多種，臺灣地處亞熱帶，常見的品種大都是比較能耐高溫的種類，以山櫻花最為常見，是臺灣最具代表性的櫻花。

目前共有68株山櫻花（又稱緋寒櫻），包括霧社種緋寒櫻、竹子湖種緋寒櫻以及重瓣緋寒櫻3種。開花期不同，霧社種及重瓣緋寒櫻的開花期二月中旬，而竹子湖種的花期較晚，通常為三月。

Taiwan Cherry Garden

Walking from the hall toward Xinyi Road, and along the waterfront walkways along the two sides at the corner gate on Hangzhou South Road, It rests the Chiang Kai-shek Memorial Hall's indigenous cheery tree area.
With the cherry being a member of the sub-genus rosaceae,
and part of the genus prunus in botany classification, The genus prunus covers 200 varieties worldwide, and is mainly distributed in the temperate areas of the northern hemisphere, of around ten varieties found in Taiwan, with Taiwan being in the subtropics, a majority of the common varieties are temperature resistant varieties,
The most common is the Formosan Cherry, and the representative one in Taiwan.

Presently there is a total of 68 Taiwan Cherry, comprising of three varieties of the Taiwan Cherry, Bamboo Lake and multiple-petal varieties. With varying flowering seasons, the Taiwan Cherry and multi-petal cherry trees bloom in mid February, while the Bamboo Lake cherry trees bloom in March.

山櫻花
學名: *Prunus campanulata* Maxim

臺灣山櫻屬於薔薇科落葉喬木，因花色緋紅寒時開，故又名緋寒櫻。葉倒卵形至長橢圓狀橢圓形，先端漸尖，葉緣具密重鋸齒，光滑。花單生或3-5朵簇生，花瓣5片，花下垂，花萼與花瓣均呈紅色。品種有深紅系的「霧社種」和粉紅色系的「竹子湖種」；盛開時全株幾乎無葉。是臺灣分佈最廣的櫻花樹種，主要分佈於全島低、中海拔闊葉林中。

Formosan Cherry
Scientific classification: *Prunus campanulata* Maxim

Taiwan's Formosan cherry is part of the Rosaceae family, an evergreen tree, and for it blooms at Kanhizakura time, it is also referred to as Kanhizakura. Leaves are ovate to elliptical, oblong, tapering at the tip, with closer serration along the edges, and smooth. The flowers are either in singles or a cluster of 3 to 5, consisting of 5 petals, with flowers dropping down, and both the calyx and petals are in red. The species include the deep-red "Wusher species" and the pink-color "Jhuzehu species"; almost leafless when in full bloom. It is the most widespread cherry tree species in Taiwan, mainly distributed in low to mid altitude broadleaf forests around the island.

綠繡眼
學名: *Zosterops japonica*

雌、雄鳥羽色特徵大致相似，不太容易用肉眼分辨。有相當醒目的白色眼圈。幾乎遍佈整個臺灣，包括城市、農村、平原、丘陵地帶與低海拔山區。喜歡群體生活。經常成小群在樹林中活動覓食，喜歡倒掛啄食果肉或昆蟲，有時會有三、四十隻以上的族群共同生活，都市公園或校園內都有其蹤跡。食物種類很多，包括植物種子、果實等，有時候也會吸食花蜜。鳴叫聲音為宏亮婉轉且細膩的『唧唧一』。

White Eye
Scientific classification: *Zosterops japonica*

The plumage of the female and male birds resembles each other, and is difficult to distinguish by naked eye. It has a prominent white circle around the eye. It is distributed nearly all around Taiwan, encompassing urban cities, farms, plains, hilly areas and low elevation mountain regions. It moves in groups. It often feeds in groups in the woods, and is fond of hooking fruit flesh or insects with its beak, and sometimes a colony of 30 to 40 birds will live together, and can be often spotted in urban parks or school campuses. It feeds on a wide variety of food, including plant seeds, fruits and such, and sometimes suckling on nectar. Its calls are loud, crisp then turn a delicate "ju ju" sound.

WONDERING
IN THE DREAMLAND
- THE BEAUTY
OF CHIANG KAI-SHEK
MEMORIAL PARK
中正紀念公園
園林之美

劉庭豪　尋夢之旅　54×39cm　2010　Liu Ting-hao　Dreamy Journey

中正紀念堂迴廊旁有許多蜿蜒曲折的小徑，置身其中，
宛如夢幻的迷宮。

Many winding paths along the halls of National Chiang Kai-shek Memorial Hall, it feels like in the dreamy labyrinth
while walking on it.

洪東標　初春　28×38cm　2010
紀念堂正後方的園林是遊客鮮少到達的地區，初春時分
山櫻花盛開，一片嫣紅映綠樹剎是美麗

Hung Tung-piao　Early Spring
The place right at the back of the National Chiang Kai-shek Memorial Hall is rarely visited by people; a charming sight created by cherry blossoms blooming in early spring and tall trees.

日本櫻花區

中正紀念公園園區內的日本櫻花為日本中央大學學員日華友好會致贈，
由93年起陸續引進，94年起定植於園區，目前園區已有200多株日本櫻花。
園區內的日本櫻花有紅華、紅笠、鬱金、花笠、關山、染井吉野、
陽光、大漁櫻、修善寺寒櫻、大寒櫻、河津櫻等11種。

Japanese Cherry Garden

The Japanese flowering cherry trees planted in the National Chiang Kai-shek Memorial Park
were bequeathed by Japan's Central University members of the Sino-Japanese Friendship
Association, which were successively brought in starting in 2004, and planted on the park
grounds starting in 2005; presently there are over 200 Japanese cherry trees planted on the
park grounds. The Japanese cherry trees planted on the park grounds consist of 11 species,
namely Prunus lannesiana Wils. cv. Kouka, Prunus lannestiana Wils. cv. Hanagasa,
Prunus lannesiana Wils. cv. Grandiflora, Prunus lannestiana Wils. cv. Sekiyama,
Prunus x yedoensis Matsum cv. Yodoensis, Prunus x campanulata cv. Yoko,
Prunus x lannesiana Wils. cv. Tairyo-zakula, Prunus x kanzakura Makino cv. Rubescenes,
Prunus x kanzakura Makino cx. Oh-kannzakura, and Prunus lannesiana Wils. cv. Kawayo-zakula.

日本櫻
學名: *Prunus spp*
園區內的日本櫻花為日本中央大學學員日華友好會致贈，由93年起陸續引進，94年起定植於園區。品種有紅華、紅笠、鬱金、花笠、關山、染井吉野、陽光、大漁櫻、修善寺寒櫻、大寒櫻、河津櫻等11種，全園區之分佈略敘如下：環堂道路大忠門側種植大寒櫻、紅笠、鬱金，環堂道路大孝門側種植修善寺寒櫻，環堂道路背面種植陽光、關山、染井吉野與大漁櫻；近雨水貯集區「友好之櫻」石碑的花圃，共種植7種日本櫻花；兩側之大草坪則種植河津櫻。

Japanese Cherry
Scientific classification: *Prunus spp*
The Japanese cherry trees planted in the garden are bequeathed by the Sino Friendship Association of Japan's Central University, and have been brought in steadily since 2004, which have been planted in the garden since 2005. The species include the Kouka, Benigasa, Grandiflora, Hanagasa, Sekiyama, Yedoensis, Yoko, Tairyo-zakula, Rubescens, Oh-kanzakura and Kawazu-zakura totaling 11 species, which are distributed throughout the garden as follows: Oh-kanzakura, Benigasa, Grandiflora are planted along the hall-encircling roadways by the Great Loyalty Gate, Rubescens is planted along the hall-encircling roadways by the the Great Piety Gate. and Yoko, Sekiyama, Yedoensis and Tairyo-zakula are planted on the backside of the hall-encircling roadways: seven Japanese cheery tree species are planted at the flowerbeds of the "Friendship cherry" stone tablet near the rainwater collecting area, and Kawazu-zakura is planted on the open lawns on two sides.

WONDERING
IN THE DREAMLAND
— THE BEAUTY
OF CHIANG KAI-SHEK
MEMORIAL PARK
中正紀念公園
園林之美

洪東標　櫻花小徑　38×56cm　2010　　Hung Tung-piao　Cherry Blossom Trail

日本友人為感念蔣公德澤特贈送櫻花造園，春天時節櫻花區一片粉紅，宛如置身北國。

For expressing the gratitude of the former President, Chiang Kai-shek, some Japanese friends send this stunning cherry blossoms garden. The pink scenery created by these beautiful cherry blossoms as if a northland.

98

謝明錩　櫻花　51×76cm　2010

冬天時，從大忠門進入中正紀念堂，可見步道兩側櫻花盛開，美不勝收。其中有緋寒櫻、吉野櫻和河津櫻等，甚至還有單瓣重瓣的不同，可謂花樣繁多。緋寒櫻又叫臺灣山櫻花，是生長於低海拔，早已適應暖和氣候的台灣原生種，一月時開花，二、三月時達到高潮，此時到中正紀念堂一定不虛此行。

Hsieh Ming-chang　Cherry Blossoms

In the winter time, the magnificent cherry blossoms flourish at both sides of trail from the entrance of the Great Loyalty Gate to the National Chiang Kai-shek Memorial Hall, including Taiwan Cherry, Prunus xyedoensis and Japanese Flowering Cherry etc of two kinds of petal, single and double, the species are quite diversified. Taiwan Cherry is also called Taiwan mountain cherry, it usually grows in the area of low altitude; while Taiwan primitive species has already adapted to the warm temperature of the island, the blossom season starts from January, fully flourish in February and March, it is worthwhile to pay a visit to the National Chiang Kai-shek Memorial Hall during its blossom period.

大忠門

由信義路進入大忠門，
花圃裡種了幾排常綠的龍柏、
與春天黃花盛開的黃花風鈴木，
馬路左側是樟樹林、原生櫻花區，
右側是竹芋科植物區、梅花林、及松樹林。

兩側的迴廊，圍繞著中正紀念公園，
提供了民眾遮風、遮陽、蔽雨的好地方，
迴廊的花窗，造形各異，
散發著中式建築的濃厚氣息。

迴廊上，有人開嗓練唱、有人練拳練武……，
有人專注凝神，彼此較量較量棋藝，
也有人只想坐坐，
三五好友聚聚聊聊，享受午後的悠閒自在。

The Great Loyalty Gate

Upon entering the Great Loyalty Gate from Xinyi Road,
A few rows of the evergreen dragon juniper and the golden trumpet-tree
that bloom with yellow flowers in the spring are planted in the flowerbeds.
To the right of the roadway are the camphor tree area and the indigenous cherry tree area,
And the right are the marantaceae area, the plum tree woods, an the pine tree woods.

The cloisters on the two sides flank the Chiang Kai-shek Memorial Hall,
providing the masses with a spot to shield from the weather elements,
The window grill along the corridors feature distinct styles
and exude a dynamic ambience of the Chinese architecture.

Along the corridors, there are people who take to practicing the vocal cord and sing,
and others take to exercising martial arts …,
Some take to meditating, and competing their skills in the chess.
And some simply take to just sitting around,
Where a group of friends hang out and chitchat, enjoying the afternoon carefree ease.

洪東標　節日的色彩　38×55cm　2010　Hung Tung-piao　Festive Color

望向大忠門，藍瓦、白牆、綠蔭和飄揚的國旗在國家節日裡洋溢熱情的景象，在母與子在漫步園區中，微風揚起青天白日滿地紅的風華

Looking over the Great Loyalty Gate, a scene full of passion made by blue tile, white walls, green shade, and flying flag in this national festival day; a boy is strolling with his mother in the garden, surrounded by the splendid glory of the national flag of TAIWAN..

WONDERING
IN THE DREAMLAND
- THE BEAUTY
OF CHIANG KAI-SHEK
MEMORIAL PARK
園林之美

林毓修　幸福　56×76cm　2010

Lin Yu-hsiu　Happiness

總在閒暇時，陪著妳逛逛園區。走累了就找個清靜的地方休息，吃著妳為我打點的餐食；不管是買的或自備，這幾十年的飲食偏好，恐怕再熟悉不過了。

愛重口味又怕血壓高、愛辣又吃不下辣，也愛在餐後來點甜食好完整一下味蕾。妳就是能在味覺享受與健康中取得平衡，這是被"心"調了味的好口感，令人百吃不膩。而妳則是在一旁靜靜地看著我陶醉的吃相。原來...『幸福』是這樣子的呀！

Used to take a little walk with you while having leisure timè, we would find a quite place to get a rest and have the foods you prepared for me, either by purchasing or made by you, during decade of years, no one knows better than you about my preference for foods.

Not easy to resist foods of heavy taste, while worrying about my high blood pressure at the same time; desire for spicy flavor but not allowed by my health condition, even a slight sweet after meal would greatly satisfy my taste bud. You are just so skilled in finding balance between delicious taste and health -- the finest taste is always made by "heart", I can never get enough from it. You just stay by my side quietly and contentedly watching me eating. so...it is the "happiness" simply desired by every one!

許德麗　光影清韻　58×76cm　2010

都説台上一分鐘台下十年功，藝術的境界來自真誠的熱愛與苦練的累積，這位大姐即使白髮飛鬢、不復年少嬌容，那鍛鍊過的姿態還是那麼美，專注的眼神告訴我們她正磨練著手上曲譜的精神，古典形窗與光影的投射讓我們一起共享那專注的片刻。

Hsu Te-li　Light, Shadow, and Clear Rhyme

People always say, one minute onstage is the hardworking of ten years offstage. The prospect of art is built on sincere enthusiasm and cumulative fruits of hardworking. Even with all the silver hair, and the beauty of youth can not be found any more, this respective lady is still highly confirmed by her long-trained skill and elegant posture; the focused expression in her eyes tells us that she is practicing the music score in her hand with her entire spirit, the classic styled window and light rejection lead us to share together this precious moment.

鄧國強　長廊　56×36cm　2010

中正紀念堂四周圍繞的長廊，甚有特色，外觀深藍色的
屋頂，顯得嚴蕭莊重，但我卻喜歡長廊的內部屋頂、牆
壁、圓柱的潔白，我用直立的構圖來畫它，利用透視來
強調它的深遠，些微的明暗、差異來畫層次，盡可能的
展現長廊的柔和、高貴、典雅，這是我畫此畫的目的。

Teng Kuo-Chang　Long Corridors

There is a particular characteristic to the long corridors surrounding the four sides of the Chiang Kai-shek Memorial Hall, with a deep blue roof that brings a touch of solemnity, yet I much prefer the whiteness of the corridor's interior roof, walls, round columns, as I try to paint it with an upright layout using a perspective view to emphasize it depth, and the minute contrast. The contrast is used to create the depth that is best to highlight the corridor's gentility, nobility and elegance, which was the purpose why I did the painting

羅淑芬　幸福　76×110 cm　2010

Luo Shu-feng　Happiness

此圖以斜對角的構圖方式，將畫面分割成對立的兩半，用以表達現實生活中理想與實際的衝突。並且使用彩色的泡泡象徵稍縱即逝的幸福。忙碌的現代人專注於工作，雖然初衷裡希望工作與休閒搭配得宜、親情與事業也能兼顧，但對工作的執著往往使理想與生活漸漸疏遠。有此體悟之後，莫要等到驚覺時光不再……；何不現在就起身走向近在咫尺的中正紀念堂，讓園區裡斑斕的陽光灑落在身上，感受那陣陣吹來的沁涼微風，張開眼就能看見親密的家人在花園裡談心，恣意的在廣場上玩耍；爺爺奶奶也來此含飴弄孫，看那專注的神情，讓我們領會到能抓住眼前的美好就是最幸福的。

This drawing uses the oblique diagonal ad composition; the picture is divided into two opposite parts, for describing the conflict between ideal and reality in our life. The colorful bubbles represent transient happiness. In the modern world, people always busy in one's career, although a balance between job and leisure is the original intention, and it would be even better to take good care of family while focusing on career; however, the ideal becomes more and more unreachable when one persists in pursuing a higher career accomplishment. With such realization in mind, we will not have to wait till it is too late to reverse an unchangeable situation…why not pay a visit to the National Chiang Kai-shek Memorial Hall now, let bright sunlight shine on you, and feel the tenderness of cool breeze. Enjoy the precious moment when watching the dearest family members chat in the garden and the carefree play of children; the satisfied expression on the face of grand parents tells us that the happiest person in the world is the one who knows how to appreciate the things one has at present.

遊園尋夢

WONDERING
IN THE DREAMLAND
– THE BEAUTY
OF CHIANG KAI-SHEK
MEMORIAL PARK
中正紀念公園
園林之美

梅花區

大忠門進入中正紀念公園的右側，即是梅花區，栽種了100多株的觀賞梅，花朵粉紅色、重瓣，花期約在2~3月間；
2棵食用梅，花朵單瓣白色、花瓣5片，12月至隔年1月開花，梅子4、5月間成熟。
另有3大棵食用梅，一棵位於大忠門入口左側原生櫻花區旁、一棵位於香草植物區內、一棵位於虎背區果樹植物區。

在這兒，雖沒白雪，但梅花盛開時的綺麗花海，為寒冬添增了濃濃春意。

在中國，雪的潔白與梅的清香相映相隨，早春梅花綻放、冬雪尚未消溶，「梅、雪爭春」之境，自古總讓文人所樂道。

北宋詩人林和靖，隱居西湖，與梅花為伴，愛梅成痴，一生不仕不娶，遂有「梅妻鶴子」的美稱，留下了千古絕唱的詠梅詩：
「眾芳搖落獨喧妍，占盡風情向小園；疏影橫斜水清淺，暗香浮動月黃昏......」；
「吟懷常恨負芳時，為見梅花輒入詩，雪後園林纔半樹，水邊籬落忽橫枝......」。

南宋·陸遊：「聞道梅花坼曉風，雪堆遍滿四山中。何方可化身千億，一樹梅花一放翁。」
......一首首詠嘆梅花的詩作，從不歇息。

梅花
學名: *Prunus mume* Sieb. et Zucc
梅花為落葉小喬木，樹幹灰褐色，小枝細長綠色無毛，
葉卵形或圓卵形，葉緣有細齒，花芽著生在長枝的葉
腋間，每節著花1~2朵，具芳香，花瓣5枚，白色至水紅，
會結果，俗稱食用梅，花期為12月至隔年1月。另有觀賞
梅，為栽培品種，有紫、紅、彩斑至淡黃等花色，多為重
瓣品種，於2月開花。

The plum tree
Scientific classification: *Prunnus mume* Sieb. et Zucc
A small deciduous tree, the plum tree is characterized
with a grayish brown tree trunk, and small twigs are
green and hairless with leaves in ovate or elliptic, with
fine teeth along the edges. Flower buds grow under
the leaf on longer branches, with 1 to 2 flowers at each
knot, which are fragrant, in a 5-petal shape, in white
to watery red, bear fruits, or so-called plums. The
flowering season spans from December to Japanese
the following year. There are also ornamental plum
trees, which are cultivated species that come in purple,
red, spots and light yellow, mostly of compound petal
species that bloom in February.

Plum Blossom Garden

To the right upon entering the Chiang Kai-shek Memorial Park through the Great Loyalty Gate is the plum Blossom Garden,
Where over 100 ornamental plum trees have been planted, with pink bloom of multi petals, which flower between February and March;
There are two plum trees with edible fruit, yielding single-petal white bloom of pentagon-shaped flowers,
which blossom from December to the following January and the plums mature between April and May.

There are also three large plum trees with edible fruit, with one located next to the Taiwan Cherry Garden by the left of the Great Loyalty Gate,
one at the Aromatic and Herbal Plants Garden, and another at the Fruit Tree Plant Garden on the right of the memorial hall grounds.

Although ostensibly missing is the snow,
yet the magnificent sea of flowers when the plum blossoms are in full bloom does add a touch of early spring to the otherwise rigid winter.

In China, as white snow is invariably accompanied by the refreshing plum blossom,
The early bloom of the plum blossoms that depicts the ushering of early spring with snow
and plum blossom before the winter snow melts never fails to capture the attention of the literary set.

The Northern Song Dynasty poet, Lin He-jing, who lived in seclusion in Xihu,
never took to court appointment or marriage for his passionate love of the plum blossom,
wanting to be surrounding by it, thus earning him the fame of having "the plum blossom as the wife and the egrets as the children",
who left behind the plum blossom sonnets that have been passed down for generations,

"Choosing to be a loner rather than joining the crowd for gaining the exclusive little garden;
reflecting through the shadows and clear water is the subtle flickering moon ..";
"Struggling to compose poetry is only inspired by the sight of the plum blossom,
crashing suddenly is a fallen trig while strolling down the gardens buried in snow ..".

The Southern Song Dynasty poet Lu Yu, "So says that plum blossom sways to the breeze, amid the snow piling all around.
Numbered in hundreds of millions, there is a carefree ease watching a plum tree blossom". ...
and there is an infinite number of poetry that glorifies the plum blossom and never seems to run dry.

竹芋科植物區

由信義路大忠門進入公園，右手邊第一個花圃即是竹芋科植物區，
竹芋的主要原產地是南美洲，部分來自非洲、印尼或澳洲等地，
原生環境在熱帶雨林區，性耐陰，所以適合榕樹林下生長。

常綠的葉片，葉柄直接從根部長出，
外觀華麗寬長，顏色和斑紋變化豐富，構成搶眼的外型，
竹芋科植物區的進駐，讓原本鬱暗的榕樹林鮮活了起來！

目前本區種植：優雅竹芋、大孔雀竹芋、孔雀竹芋、浪心竹芋、
箭尾竹芋、豔錦竹芋、斑葉竹芋、大紅羽竹芋、紅羽竹芋、
葛鬱金、蘭嶼竹芋......等十幾種。
葛鬱金，原產於加勒比海地區，俗名叫做粉薯，
其塊莖可提取澱粉，是製造太白粉的材料來源；
肖竹芋屬的一些種類，葉上的斑紋十分美麗，常做為室內觀賞植物，
成株於夏、秋季開花，花梗自葉叢中抽生，穗狀或圓錐花序。

Marantaceae Plant Garden

Entering the park through the Great Loyalty Gate on Xinyi Road,
to the right of the first garden ground is the Marantaceae Plant Garden.
The arrowroots primarily thrive in South America, with some coming from Africa, Indonesia, Australia and such,
In an indigenous growth environment in the tropical rainforests, it is shade resistant, and growing ideally under the banyan trees.

With evergreen leaves, and the leaf stems growing right from the roots,
It has a ornate, elongated appearance, and an eye-catching appearance for its coloration and spot variations.
The marataceae plant area adds a touch of vibrancy to the otherwise dark banyan tree woods.

The varieties planted in the area include the Calathea leopardina, Calathea roseopicta, Calathea makoyana E. Merr,
Calathea rufibara, Calathea insignis, Calathea oppenheimiana cv. Quadricilor, Calathea zebrina, Calathea sanderiana,
Calathea sanderiana, Maranta arundinacea L., Maranthaceae.
Prayer plant, initially thrives in the Caribbean region, and is commonly known as rhizome, a fleshy root

The tubers can be extracted of starch, a source for making the starch mix;
Some of the varieties in maranta boast rather appealing spot patterns on the leaves,
and are often used as indoor ornamental plants.
With grown plants blooming in the summer and autumn,
the flower stalks shoot up from the leaf clusters in a cluster or cone-shaped inflorescence.

萵鬱金
學名: *Maranta arundinaceae* L.

別名竹竽、金筍、芝粉、粉薯或紫薯，原產於熱帶中南美洲及西印度群島。植株於秋冬季落葉休眠，利用休眠期間採收其地下部膨大塊莖，地下塊莖是製造太白粉的澱粉原料，其他肖竹芋屬的一些種類，葉子上有美麗的斑紋，常被栽培做室內植物觀賞。成株於夏、秋季開花，花梗自葉叢中抽生，為穗狀或圓錐花序。

The maranta starch or arrowroot
scientific classification: *Maranta arundinaceae* L.

Also known as arrowroot, golden bamboo, maranta powder or purple starch, it is originated in tropic Central and South America and West Indies. The plants become dormant in the fall and winter, as the rhizomes expand in size underground; the subcutaneous rootstock is the ingredient used to produce starch. Other maranta family species have attractive patterns on the leaves, and are often cultivated as indoor ornamental plants. The grown plants bloom in the summer and fall, with flower stems extend from the leaf cluster, in a cluster or funnel inflorescence.

蘭嶼竹芋
學名: *Donax canniformis* (Forst. f.) Rolfe

多年生亞灌木狀直立草本。莖具分枝，分枝基部有一舌狀苞片，葉生於分枝上部，單葉互生，卵狀長橢圓形，全緣，光滑，羽狀脈明顯，先端有一銳尖頭，葉鞘抱莖。花成對，頂生、疏散的圓錐花序。蘭嶼地區的人用枝幹來編製籃子等器具。分布於蘭嶼，較潮濕之次生林中，為台灣唯一原生之竹芋科植物。

Cannalike Dona
Scientific classification: *Donax canniflrmis* (Forst. f.) Rolfe

A small, perennial shrub, it is an upright herb. The base splits and contains a tongue bract, with leaves grown on the top part of the branch, of single leaf in alternate growth, ovate or elliptical, full edge and smooth, visible vines, a sharp tip at the edge, with leaf sheaths enveloping the stem. Flowers grow in pair, at the topside, of a sparse funnel inflorescence. Residents of Lan Yu use the tree trunk for basket weaving and other utensils. It is distributed on the Orchid Island, in moist secondary forests, and is the only endemic maranta in Taiwan.

WONDERING
IN THE DREAMLAND
– THE BEAUTY
OF CHIANG KAI-SHEK
MEMORIAL PARK
中正紀念公園
園林之美

王瀚賢　歇息　51×76cm　2010　　　　Wang Han-Shien　Resting

漫步於雲漢池旁與步道兩側皆有許多造型奇特的石頭，
其中常見三、五或成群麻雀跳躍於石間，麻雀彼此姿態
各異，而鳥語此起彼落好不熱鬧，形成一幅生動有趣的
景象。

There are many uniquely shaped boulders on both sides the walking trails by the Yuhan Pool, and walking on
the trail one sees three to five or groups sparrows wandering around the boulders, where the sparrows appears
in different plumages, and a cacophony of chirping sounds come to frame an engaging and playful image.

林毓修　坐下來看個報吧！　56×76cm　2010　Lin Yu-Hsiu　Why not sit down and relax a while!

花了大半輩子的忙碌，總有步履停不住的無奈。退休後的日子，頓時多了些許空白與停滯。沒了上班時的擠壓、更少了上司那緊迫盯人的模樣。上午十點半...有的是三份報紙的陪伴與一種恣意的滿足。
身在車水馬龍的台北，生活一直緊張地跟隨。這鬧區中難得的綠帶，何不試著停下腳步，找個蔭涼處坐下來，翻開報紙看看時事、瞧瞧股市、了解一下現今的世界；當然也適時地讓自己放鬆放鬆，享受這片刻的愜意吧！

After busing for over a half of whole life, I feel even unable to stop for a moment; the life after retirement seems nothing but emptiness and blank. No pressure in neither office nor the eyes of superior fixing on the back; ten and half in the morning...three copies of newspapers and a carefree satisfaction are now my companies.
Trapped in the heavy traffic of Taipei, life tensely goes on without an exit. A precious green in an chaotic urban area, why not try to stop a while and find a shady place to cool down; better understand the current world by reading newspaper, new information, stock market etc. Just relax and enjoy the momentary leisure!

WONDERING
IN THE DREAMLAND
—THE BEAUTY
OF CHIANG KAI-SHEK
MEMORIAL PARK
中正紀念公園
園林之美

光華池

暢遊了一圈綠臂彎的花叢綠園，
在光華池畔，悠閒地停下腳步……。

欣賞著，
小白鷺，專注凝視池水的身影；
翠鳥，筆直衝入水中的獵魚絕技；
紅冠水雞與鯉魚爭食，飼料緊含口中，
急游回巢哺育幼鳥，來回無數次的奔波；
以及台東火刺木滿樹鮮紅的小圓果，邀來群鳥的盛宴……。

天的藍、橋的白、垂柳的黃綠、音樂廳的橙紅……，
從日出到月明星稀……，
時間與季節的推移，讓水色變幻出一幅幅美妙的畫面。

池畔的景緻，落入池水調色盤，
邊界交融、模糊了，細節減少了，卻增添了輕鬆與溫柔，
看著、看著，
心中的紛亂，也隨之溶化、沉靜了……。

瑣事的鑽研，帶來無盡的煩惱，
緩一緩、歇一歇吧，
讓池水，為心靈注入一份舒暢與浪漫！

碧綠清澈的雙眼 「光華池、雲漢池」，
在城市的綠洲中輕輕哼唱！

【光華池：位於信義路旁，緊臨音樂廳。「光華」為光復中華之意，池面積約三千平方公尺，為不規則形狀的人工池，配以人造假山、瀑布及白色半圓形拱橋，景緻十分優美。】

Guanghua Pond

After visiting the whole area of greenish flowering shrubs,
it's nice to stop by the Guanghua Pond leisurely and enjoy the scenery.

There are Little Egrets staring at their shadow in the water
and the Common Kingfisher plunge dive into water for preying.
Common Moorhen and carps fight for the feeding stuff,
fetch and feed to the young.
There are also flocks of birds attracted by the small round fruits
of Taitung Firethorn.

The blue of sky, white of the bridge, leaf-green of willow and the salmon
of the concert hall all change with the seasons from sunrise to sunset.
These all compose lots of different fantastic pictures.

The scenery by the pond reflects on the water just as the palette
which portrays the nature in a relaxing and gentle way without the details.
When looking at the natural painting,
the tumults and worries would just disappear...

Let go all the trifles and take a break with the scenery by the pond;
let the water and the nature balance your mind
and soul in a romantic way.

The clean and greenish Guanghua Pond and Yunhan Pond
are like the two beautiful eyes crooning softly by this city oasis.

Guanghua Pond is right next to the Natronal Concert Hall by Xinyi Road.
"Guanghua" means Taiwan Restoration in Chinese. The area of the pond is about
3000 square meters which is an artificial pond in irregular shape. The pond is
decorated with artificial mountains, man-made waterfalls, and white arch bridges.
It's extremely beautiful.

小白鷺
學名: *Egretta garzetta*
全身羽色雪白而修長。嘴、腳皆為黑色，腳趾為明顯的黃綠色。繁殖期眼先轉為紅色，頭、枕部後方有兩根長飾羽，非繁殖期則無飾羽。在臺灣為常見之留鳥，主要分布從平地至低海拔之溪流、水田、魚塭、沼澤、河口、沙洲地帶，部份冬季會南遷。飛行時常發出「嘎嘎」之沙啞喉音。會以腳探入水中擾動，捕食受驚嚇四竄的魚蝦。繁殖期與其他鷺科鳥類集體築巢於竹林、相思樹及木麻黃等樹上。

Little Egret
Scientific classification: *Egretta garzetta*
It has a white plumage and a slender built. With its beak and feet being black, its toe webs are in a noticeable green/yellow hue. At the mating season, it first turns red, and two ornamental features begin to appear behind the head and the neck, but not visible during the non-mating season. A sedentary bird often seen in Taiwan, it is primarily distributed in rivers and creeks, wet rice paddies, fishponds, swamps, tributaries, shovels from flatlands to low altitude areas, and some will migrate to the south in winter months. It often emits a scratchy, throaty sound. It tends to roughen the water with its foot to capture fish and shrimps running scared. During the mating season, it builds collective nests with other birds in the egret family on trees such as bamboo growth, acacias and ironwoods.

翠鳥
學名: *Alcedo atthis*
以捕食魚類為主。經常靜立水域旁突出的枝頭、岩石上低頭搜尋獵物，發現獵物即快速衝入水中捕食，有時也會在空中定點振翅，搜尋魚蹤，再陡降衝入水中抓魚。亦獵食蛙類、小型爬蟲及昆蟲。翅膀短小，以直線方式飛行，飛行時常發出『嘰』般的鳴聲。

Common Kingfisher
Scientific classification: *Alcedo atthis*
It mainly feeds on fish. Often perches quietly on branches extending over the water or rocks searching for pray, and quickly dives into the water to catch the pray when spotting one, and sometimes flaps its wings at a fixed aerial position looking for traces of the fish before diving into the water to catch it. Also feeds on frogs, small reptiles and insects. With rather short wings, it flies in a linear manner, and often emits a screeching call when flying.

WONDERING
IN THE DREAMLAND
– THE BEAUTY
OF CHIANG KAI-SHEK
MEMORIAL PARK
中正紀念公園
園林之美

垂柳
學名: *Salix babylonica* Linn.

落葉喬木,幹粗大,樹皮深灰色,小枝細長,柔軟而下垂。垂柳易以扦插繁殖,選成熟而未老化之枝條,在葉片脫落新芽未抽出前扦插容易成活。葉互生,線狀披針形或狹披針形,先端銳尖或漸尖,基部銳尖或漸尖,紙質,表面呈有光澤綠色而背面為白粉狀,葉緣有細鋸齒,幼時有短柔毛,然後表裡兩面皆光滑無毛;托葉歪卵至披針形。雌雄異株,葇荑花序,無花序梗或近似無花序。

Weeping willow
Scientific classification: *Salix babylonica* Linn.

A deciduous tree, it has large tree trunk, a dark grayish bark, with slender and long branches that are soft and drape pendulously. The Babylon willows are easy to propagate by grafting, and the chances of survival improve when grafting mature, healthy branches when the leaves have fallen off before the new shoots emerge. Leaves are grown alternately, in linear needle shaped leaves, taping to a slightly sharp tip, and the base is pointy or slightly pointy, of a paper texture, with surface sheen, green on the front and powdery white on the back, serration along the edges of the leaf, with soft hair on tender leaves, but mature to hairless on both sides; the stipules are a skewed ovate or elliptic. Dioecious, it either has a panicle inflorescence, non-inflorescence of a pseudo non-inflorescence.

灰背蘇鐵小灰蝶
學名: *Chilades pandava peripatria*

又名蘇鐵小灰蝶、東陸蘇鐵小灰蝶,幼蟲以臺灣蘇鐵、蘇鐵等嫩葉為食,如果你看到葉片被啃食得亂七八糟的鐵樹,就是蘇鐵小灰蝶幼蟲們的傑作。雄蝶背面有耀眼的紫色,雌蝶則在黑褐色的底色上著有一片湛藍色的鱗粉,這片湛藍色的鱗粉會隨著季節有不同變化。臺灣的蘇鐵小灰蝶是臺灣特有亞種,但它卻遲至一九八九年才被命名記載。

Cycad Blue Butterfly
Scientific classification: *Chilades pandava peripatria*

Also known as the blue butterfly, rising blue butterfly, its larvae feed on the tender shoots of the Formosan cycads or cycads, and if you see the center of a Fissidens Iron being messed up, you can be sure that it was the work of the cycad blue butterfly's larvae. The male butterfly as a brilliant purple back, while the female has a gleaming blue scale powder on a black background, where the blue changes color along the season. Taiwan's cycad blue butterfly is an endemic infraorder in Taiwan, but it has only been named and documented as late as by 1989.

台東火刺木
學名: *Pyracantha koidzumii* (Hayata) Rehd.

屬常綠性灌木,小枝尖端成刺狀,葉互生,在短枝上簇生,長橢圓形,先端微凹,略反捲。花白色五瓣,聚繖花序,盛開時像有滿株的積雪。果扁球形,成熟時豔紅亮麗,盛產可達數千粒,成熟時極為美麗壯觀。性喜高溫,耐旱,日照需充足。這些可愛的小果實不僅可以欣賞,還可以釀酒,甚至可以磨成粉代替米糧,是戰亂期間的救荒糧食,在大陸有「救兵糧」的別稱。

Taitung Firethorn
Scientific classification: *Pyracantha koidzumii* (Hayata) Rehd.

An evergreen shrub, it has small branches in a thorny configuration, leaves grow alternate, clustering on short branches, in oblong shape, with the tips slightly curved down. The flowers are white, in five petals, a clustering, tender inflorescence, and blooms to resemble a snow-covered plant. Fruits are flat spheres, mature to a bright red gloss, which can number to thousands in full swing, offering a majestic view. Thrives in heat, draught resistant, and needs ample sunlight. These adorable fruits are more than ornamental but can be used for making alcohol, or even ground to powder as a substitute of grain; a life-saving staple in wartimes, thus the nickname, the "salvation grain", in mainland China.

柯衛光　光華池　19.7×54.6cm　2010　**Ke Wei-guang　Guanghua Pond**

二十年前來台北就讀，借居東門，因地緣關係，一週必
訪三次以上中正紀念堂。
經由本次深度遊園才知，光華池與國家音樂廳中間步
道，延伸到雲漢池與國家戲劇院，劃分為兩單位管理。
本以為整個圍牆內皆為中正紀念堂管理處管理。

I visited at least three times the National Chiang Kai-shek Memorial Hall while studying in Taipei twenty years ago since
I lived in the nearby neighborhood, the East Door.
From this garden deep exploration did I learned that trail between Guanghua Pond and the National Concert Hall extends
till the Yunhan Pond and the National Theater, the area is divided into two parts and governed by two different units;
I thought the whole area inside the enclosing wall is under the authority of National Chiang Kai-shek Memorial Hall.

WONDERING
IN THE DREAMLAND
- THE BEAUTY
OF CHIANG KAI-SHEK
MEMORIAL PARK
中正紀念公園
園林之美

劉淑美　你走近-光華池　　76×56cm　　2010　　Liu Sue-mei　When you come close to - Guanghua Pond

夏日池水予人忘憂，我恣意要池水一片白靜，只輕掃水色滑過寧靜午后。鳶尾是池間駐足的紫蝶，我欣然…………

The pond water in summer soothe and relieve the worry...I capriciously demand complete clear and serenity of pond water; it only touches the tranquil afternoon by slightly stroking the water surface. The iris is the place residing purple butterfly, I'm gladly...

蔡秀雅　國家音樂廳　38×56cm　2010　Tsai Hsiu-ya　National Concert Hall

午後在這炙熱的炎夏裡，
魚兒暢快的在池間悠遊；
有交錯的樹影為我遮陰、
和微風帶來些許的清涼，
享盡此刻的寧靜與優閒。

In this hot summer afternoon,
Cheerfully swimming in the pools is fish;
Interlacing shadows hide me from heat and tiredness,
The soft breeze soothes me with its cool,
Enjoy the tranquility and leisure only at this moment.

WONDERING
IN THE DREAMLAND
— THE BEAUTY
OF CHIANG KAI-SHEK
MEMORIAL PARK
中正紀念公園
園林之美

陳樹業　光華池邊的楊木　39×54cm　2010

光華池是不規則形狀的人工池，配以人造假山，半圓形拱橋、
小瀑布及池內飼養各色各樣紋彩斑爛的錦鯉，水池周圍種植許
多榕樹、楊木、松柏…等，兩兩三三散步的人經過羊腸小道，
踏過綠影，環湖觀賞寧靜美好的園地。作者描繪此景是斜光罩
著楊木光影變化多采多姿，倒影與水波相映，景觀特殊，十分
優美，不勝引人陶醉。

Chen Su-yen　The Poplar Trees by the Guanghua Pond

The Guanghua Pond is of an irregular-shaped artificial pond, coordinated with artificial faux rocks,
arched bridge, small waterfall, and houses a host of brilliantly colored carps, and around the edge of
the pond planted many banyan trees, poplars, pines and so forth, where people in pairs or threes walk
leisurely pas the winding footpath, traversing the green shadows and taking in the fine gardens through
the water reflections. The creator depicts the shadows of light passing through the poplar woods with
a magnificent touch, where the reversed shadows are reflected with the ripples of the water, creating a
unique landscape and a touch of enchanting elegance.

吳冠德　池畔暮色　39×54cm　2010　Wu Guan-de　Pond Dusk

日暮時分，優雅的白橋映出美麗的倒影，落日墜入池中，如詩如畫。

During the dusk time, the elegant white bridge mirrors its beautiful reflection in the water, where is the sunset falling into; the enchanting sight is like a picture.

WONDERING
IN THE DREAMLAND
- THE BEAUTY
OF CHIANG KAI-SHEK
MEMORIAL PARK
中正紀念公園
園林之美

大廣場

久戀　文明　燈紅　濃濃蜜蜜，
灰色　暗沉　狹擠　憂憂茫茫，
自錮的心　等待　等待　開啟......！

天地　浩浩瀚瀚　寬寬闊闊，
讓心房解了鎖，
如鷫鵒　如群鴿，
奔向草綠綠　飛向天藍藍.....！

躺仰　靜賞　雲在飄，
闔眼　輕聞　花在香，
微風　輕柔
發了呆　打個盹，
尋回甜甜淨淨的兒時夢！

Main Plaza

Lingering, the civilization, lights red, and there is a savory sensation,
Gray in color, dark, crowded, there is a sense of trepidation,
The self-inflicted heart awaits and waits to be opened!

The heaven and earth, which are wide and open, they unleash the heart, just like the egrets
and just like the pigeons, they embrace toward the green and soar to the blue skies!

Lying still, and watching the clouds float by,
Closing the eyes, smelling gently of the fragrant flowers,
The breeze blows gently,
Have some idle thoughts and doze off a little,
Time to recapture the sweet and pure childhood dreams!

家燕
學名：*Hirundo rustica*

嘴小、頭大，雙翼尖長，體背黑色有藍色金屬光澤。額、喉紅褐色，上胸有黑色橫帶。在臺灣為普遍的夏候鳥，部分為九月至翌年四月的冬候鳥。七月至九月為主要過境時期，數量相當龐大。喜愛停棲於平地至低海拔之人工建物及電線上。通常大群飛翔於城市、鄉村、農耕地、草原、河床或海邊等上空。習性偏好群居活動，飛行能力很強，能巧妙地翻轉飛行。飛行中會邊飛邊鳴唱，鳴叫聲為「啾、啾」，並覓食空中的小蚊蟲。

Barn swallow
Scientific classification: *Hirundo rustica*

Small peak, large head, it has slender wings and black back with metallic blue sheen. The head and throat are in a reddish brown hue, and a lateral black band around the neck. A common summer migratory bird in Taiwan, and some are winter migratory birds between September and April of the following year. The time between July and September is the main migratory period, moving in enormous numbers. It likes to perch on artificial buildings and electric poles on flatlands to low-lying areas. Large flocks of the barn swallow often fly above cities, countryside, farmland, grasslands, riverbeds, and by the seashore. Gravitate toward moving in groups, it is a dynamic flyer and can flip midair. It emits a "ju ju" sound while flying, and feeds on small insects and mosquitoes in midair.

珠頸斑鳩
學名：*Streptopelia chinensis*

體型中型，雌、雄鳥羽色特徵大致相似，不容易用肉眼分辨。前額、頰部與頭頂灰色，喉部到腹部為栗紅色，腳紅色。經常單獨或成小群在地面上活動覓食。食物種類很多，包括植物種子、果實、穀類等，有時候也會啄食一些嫩葉及果實也是覓食的對象。鳴叫聲音為重複的『咕—咕—咕—』，常在清晨鳴叫，可連續好幾分鐘。

Spotted-necked Dove
Scientific classification: *Streptopelia chinensis*

A mid-size built, the plumage of the male and female resemble each other, thus difficult to tell by naked eye. The forehead, cheeks and top of the head are in gray, and the throat down to the belly is in red, with red feet. It often forages on the grounds alone or in groups. Omnivorous, it forages on plant seeds, fruit, grain and such, and sometimes pecks on tender leaves and fruit. It calls in a 'gu, gu' sound, often early in the morning, lasting for several minutes.

WONDERING
IN THE DREAMLAND
- THE BEAUTY
OF CHIANG KAI-SHEK
MEMORIAL PARK
中正紀念公園
園林之美

鴿子
學名: *Columba livia*

臺北都會地區觀察到數量最多的是在二重疏洪道附近及中正紀念公園，目前統計大臺北地區數量約有超過二千隻。在臺灣野外落地生根群聚地生活，繁殖場域尋找到與其祖先岩鴿野外生存環境相似的地方--『高樓大廈』，這些地方與野外的懸崖峭壁一樣，適合它們繁殖及棲息。因為常築巢或棲息在窗台、冷卻水塔、冷氣機之中，羽毛以及乾掉的糞便灰塵，都會飄進室內，會有傳佈病菌以及造成過敏的機會，對日常生活已有一定程度的不良影響。

Pigeon
Scientific classification: *Columba livia*

The areas around the Erzhong flood canals and the Chiang Kai-shek Memorial Park provide a vantage point for pigeon watching in the greater Taipei area, which according to the current statistics numbered to around 2,000 in the greater Taipei area. They thrive and live in clusters in the wilderness of Taiwan, and search for habitats that resemble the survival environment of their ancestral rock pigeons - the "high rise buildings". These places provide the same steep cliffs, ideal for them to inhibit and mate. With their building nests or perching on windowsills, nesting around cooling towers and air-conditioning units, the fine feathers and dust of the droppings can be circulated indoors to spread the bacteria and allegiants, which more or less pose certain threat to the human activity.

鶺鴒
學名: *Motacilla spp.*

全世界共5屬51種，常見的有白鶺鴒、灰鶺鴒、黃鶺鴒及日本鶺鴒。其體型都是細細長長的，站著時身體與地面平行，後面拖著長長窄窄的尾巴，時常上下擺動。區分如下：1.白鶺鴒：全身為醒目的黑白兩色，冬、夏羽色略有不同。2.灰鶺鴒：頭至背部為鼠灰色，尾羽黑色，外側白色，有白色眉斑，腹部黃色，腿黃褐色。3.黃鶺鴒：頭至背部黃綠色，腹黃色，眉斑白色或黃色，冬羽時背部呈灰褐色，腿黑色。4.日本鶺鴒：頭至頸部及上胸皆為黑色，僅額、眉斑及腮白色；背部之黑色部分終年皆為黑色。

Wagtail
Scientific classification: *Motacilla spp.*

There are five geniuses, 51 varieties around the world, and those commonly seen are the white pelican, gray pelican, yellow pelican and Japanese pelican. They shall share a slender built, stand parallel to the ground, with a narrow tail trailing in the back, swaying occasionally up and down. Their distinctions are as follows: 1. The white pelican: the entire body has a black and white plumage, which varies in the summer and winter. 2. The gray pelican: it has a mousy gray hue on the head to the black, with black tail feathers, white on the outside, with two white brow spots, yellow belly and yellowish brown legs. 3. The yellow pelican: it has a yellowish green hue from the head to the back, yellow belly, with white or yellow brow spots, black on the legs; the back turns a grayish brown hue in winter plumage. 4. The Japanese pelican: It has a black hue from the head to the upper chest, but white on the forehead, brow spots and cheeks, and the black on the back remains black all-year-round.

周嘉成　餵鴿子　38×55cm　2010

Zhou Jia-cheng　Feeding the Pigeons

午後的陽光絢麗而耀眼，人們在自由廣場前輕鬆的散步，偶有停下腳步的遊客，拿起手中的麵包餵起鴿子。鴿子，廣場和遊客，突然間相映成一幅浪漫的圖畫。

Amid the brilliant and glaring afternoon sun,people walk leisurely in front of the liberty Square, with some occasionally stopping their pace, and others turn to feeding the pigeons with the bread in their hands. The pigeons, the plaza, and the visitors suddenly converge into a romantic image.

李曉寧　仙丹　56×75cm　2008

異常的氣候讓七、八月的臺北像個大蒸籠，驕陽下的行人個個汗流浹背，花草也經不起酷曬而顯得垂頭喪氣，反觀仙丹卻是生氣盎然，一團團叢聚在一起像顆小火球，像是在和太陽較勁，陽光愈大愈是開花，花色愈是耀眼，為這慵懶的夏天增添活潑的氣息。

Lee Hsiao-ning　Ixora chinensis

In July and August, Taipei is a true steamer due to the global abnormal climate; people sweat under the blazing sun, even the plants and flowers lose their vitality and wither easily; even so, the Ixora chinensis still vigorously bloom in cluster, as groups of little red balls, contending with the powerful sun. The fiercer the sun is, the more they bloom, and the color becomes even more brilliant, adding enormous vivacity to this idle summer.

林玉葉　綻放　76×56cm　2010
黃澄澄的花朵，個個碩大飽滿，像音符在跳躍，奔
放的花瓣有著書法流暢的筆意，綻放盎然的生命。

Lin Yu-yeh　Blossom
The bright yellow flowers gorgeously bloom, as joyfully dancing musical notes; a fluent smoothness of calligraphy writing brush hidden in the vivacious petals, as a thriving vivid life.

「中華亞太水彩藝術協會」簡介

有鑑於國內水彩畫曾經於八十年代的畫壇有著輝煌之表現，而在當今畫壇間卻日漸勢微，多有感觸，為了提昇國內創作水準與改善創作環境，國內幾位水彩專業創作人士在經過多方的徵詢意見後，決定比照水彩先進國家的組織模式，組成一個新的優質繪畫團體，於2005年正式向內政部申請合法立案為「中華亞太水彩藝術協會」。以宣揚水彩藝術，推動全民藝術運動，促進水彩成為國民美術為宗旨。

協會成立以來，以嚴謹之幹部任期制、會員分級制、會員限額制暨升級審核制度來建立會員之榮譽感並確保創作之水平。「中華亞太水彩藝術協會」集結當代老中青專精於水彩創作的畫家組成，依據章程必須以具有全國性大賽水彩類前三名得獎記錄及大學水彩課教師資格者方能成為正式會員，現有「正式會員」、「准會員」、「預備會員」、等九十餘人；協會參考英國皇家水彩協會的模式，以年度創作的作品表現及參展競賽成績作為會員升等的審核標準，這樣的分級制乃建立在榮譽與責任的理念，提昇創作水平和鼓勵畫家參與水彩創作的積極目的。

會務以舉辦展覽、創作研討、寫生觀摩、專題講座、推廣教育等活動為主，並以成為創作與學術研究並重的專業團體為目標，進而結合政府與民間力量共同舉辦主題性水彩展覽、水彩大賽、發表學術研究專籍等，藉此團結水彩畫壇以共創良好的創作空間與環境。

協會自成立以來已辦理多項國內重大活動，2006年四月與國立歷史博物館合辦「風生水起-國際華人水彩經典大展」暨「國際華人水彩創作與教育研討會」，並邀請中國美術家協會水彩藝術委員會黃鐵山主席與委員等共十人來台進行學術與創作研討交流；2006年十一月應邀參與慶祝中山樓建樓四十週年在國父紀念館展出「中山樓百景」大展； 2007年為慶祝玉山國家公園管理處處慶應邀展出「河海山林」水彩特展；2007慶祝國父紀念館建館五十週年應邀參與展出「國父紀念館百景」大展；2008與農委會林業試驗所合辦「台灣的森林」水彩巡迴五所大學特展，並接續為台灣七所植物園進行寫生與出版水彩專輯等；與歷史博物館合辦2008「台灣水彩一百年大展」及為紀念台灣水彩百年在中正紀念堂舉辦「臺灣當代全國水彩大展」等，2009年與連江縣政府、中正紀念堂合辦「馬祖百景大展」；與新竹市政府合辦「印象風城」水彩展等，為推廣水彩藝術，2010年舉辦「兩岸水彩交流展暨創作研討會」；為慶祝中正紀念堂成立30週年策展「遊園尋夢-中正園區之美水彩展」等；並計畫於2011年建國100年策展「國家植物園之美水彩大展」及「建國百年全國水彩大展」等；協會也自2007年起開始發行「水彩藝術資訊」雜誌，以免費提供讀者；這些重大展出和出版活動為提升國內水彩創作的風氣與水平發揮極大作用，未來期使水彩在國內大受歡迎，而本會已成為國內最受肯定與尊重的藝術團體。

Introduction of Chinese Asia Pacific Watercolor Art Association

In view of watercolor paintings' flourishing development in Taiwan in the 80s and diminished popularity in recent years, several professional watercolor artists have decided to follow lawsuit of advanced nations in order to provide an environment for creativity. In 2005, Chinese Asia Pacific Watercolor Art Association duly approved by the Ministry of the Interior was established to propagandize watercolor art and promote "art for all" nationwide.

Since its establishment, "the cadres' term of office', "member categorization", "member limit", and "membership upgrade review" were implemented to foster members' sense of honor and maintain high standards. The association comprises of young, middle-aged, and senior watercolor painters. To qualify as full membership members, they must be top three winners at watercolor contests and watercolor instructors in colleges/universities. Currently, there are 90 "full membership", "prospective membership", and "associate membership" members. The membership upgrade review is conducted in a similar manner as that of the Royal Watercolors Society to foster members' sense of honor and responsibility, improve creation standards, and elicit painters'active participation in watercolor creations.

The association is a creation and academic research based professional organization that holds exhibitions, creation seminars, outdoor sketching, topic seminars, and education promotion. Topic watercolor exhibitions, watercolor contests, and academic research presentations are also jointly held with the government and private sector in order to integrate the watercolor circle and provide an excellent creation environment.

During early establishment, major events have been held such as "The Wind Rises; the Water Ascends: 2006 International Exhibition of Classics of Chinese Watercolorists" and "Chinese Watercolorists' Creation and Education seminar' jointly held by National Museum of History in 2006, Chinese Artists' Association Watercolor Art Committee Chairman Huang Tie-shan and members' academic and creation seminar exchange, the 44th "One Hundred Views of Chungshan Hall Exhibition" held at the National Dr. Sun Yat-sen Memorial Hall in November 2006, the 50th "River, Sea, Mountain, and Forest" Watercolor Exhibition in celebration of the 50th Anniversary of the National Dr. Sun Yat-sen's Memorial Hall in 2007, "Taiwan's Forest" Watercolor Tour Special Exhibition jointly held by Taiwan Forestry Research Institute at five universities in 2008, outdoor sketching, special watercolor editions for seven botanical gardens, the 2008 Centennial Watercolor Exhibition in Taiwan, the "National Contemporary Watercolor Exhibition in Taiwan". In 2009 collaborated 'Battleground Bells-Paintings The Beautiful Scenery of The Matus Islands' with Lienchiang County Government and the Chiang Kai-shek Memorial Hall, and also 'Impression of the Wind City' with the Hsinchu City Government to promote the watercolor art. In 2010, in order to promote cross-strait watercolor painting exchanges and learn by the vigorous development in China in recent years, we held '2010 Cross-strait Exhibition of Watercolors by Famous Painters and seminar' ; For celebrating the 30th anniversary of National Chiang Kai-shek Memorial Hall, we held the "Wondering in the dreamland – The beauty of Chiang Kai-shek Memorial Park" Watercolor Exhibitions. We scheme out the "Major Watercolor Exhibition on the Beauty of the National Botanical Gardens" and the "Major Watercolor Exhibition for the Centennial National Founding Celebration" among other exhibitions in 2011 to celebrate the centennial national founding of Taiwan. The association has published Watercolor News Update (free of charge) since 2007 to maintain local watercolor creation standards and is a well-known prestigious arts group that continues to set the trend.

遊園尋夢
WONDERING
IN THE DREAMLAND
— THE BEAUTY
OF CHIANG KAI-SHEK
MEMORIAL PARK
中正紀念公園
園林之美

陳樹業 Chen Su-Yeh　1930

現職　苗栗縣美術協會常務理事、專業畫家

學歷　國立師範大學美術學系國訓班結業
　　　台中師專畢業

經歷　1968 任苗栗縣立大湖國民中學美術教師
　　　1980 任苗栗縣美術協會理事長二屆
　　　1989 任苗栗私立育民高職學校美術教師

獲獎　建國六十年全省書畫展西畫類第一名
　　　第二十九屆全省美展水彩畫第二名
　　　第三十屆全省美展水彩畫第三名
　　　第二十五、二十六屆全省美展水彩畫優選獎
　　　1964.1966.1967 年全省教員美展水彩畫優選獎
　　　教育部國家文藝水彩類優選獎
　　　韓國文化大賞美展西畫類優選獎
　　　台灣省61年度教學優良教師受教育廳長獎
　　　台灣省70年度特殊優良教師受教育廳長獎（師鐸獎）

畫歷　全省美展40.50年回顧展邀請於台中省立美術館展出。
　　　第一屆至第五屆中.韓.日美術交流展於台北、東京、漢城
　　　展出、
　　　中、美、澳三國水彩畫聯展於台北中正畫廊展出。
　　　第一屆至十四屆亞洲水彩畫聯盟展於台、日、韓、馬、
　　　泰、港、印展出。
　　　國際華人水彩經典大展邀請於歷史博物館展出。
　　　韓國國際水彩大展於首爾展出。
　　　2007 河海山林專題展。
　　　2008 紀年台灣水彩百年當代、水彩大展、台灣森林之美
　　　　　　水彩巡迴特展。
　　　2009 台北植物園詩畫聯展於中正畫廊展出
　　　　　　新竹印象風城水彩展於新竹文化中心展出
　　　2010「戰地鐘聲」馬祖列島百景大展
　　　　　　「水彩的壯闊波濤」兩岸水彩名家交流大展
　　　　　　「遊園尋夢」中正紀念公園園林之美水彩展

鄧國強 Teng Kuo-Chiang　1934

現職　專業畫家
　　　中華亞太水彩藝術協會常務監事
　　　水彩藝術資訊雜誌總編輯

學歷　政治作戰學校美術系畢
　　　台灣大學中文系畢

獲獎　中國畫協會金爵獎

畫歷　1985-2002 共個展7次
　　　2002 臺灣師範大學圖書館藝文空間個展、
　　　2004 玉山風華國-玉山國家公園百景展於歷史博物館
　　　2006 風生水起-國際華人水彩藝術大展於歷史博物館
　　　2007 國父紀念館德明藝廊個展
　　　　　　河海山林專題展（玉山國家公園）
　　　2008 紀念臺灣水彩百年當代2008水彩大展
　　　　　　「臺灣意象---櫻花鉤吻鮭暨雪霸百景」主題展
　　　　　　臺灣森林之美水彩巡迴特展
　　　　　　臺灣民主百景百位名家藝術聯展
　　　　　　塔塔加至玉山主峰步道之美水彩展
　　　　　　（玉山國家公園）
　　　2008 台灣水彩一百年大展
　　　2009「福山之美」水彩特展
　　　2009 台北植物園詩畫聯展
　　　2009「印象風城」水彩展
　　　2010「戰地鐘聲」馬祖列島百景大展
　　　　　　「水彩的壯闊波濤」兩岸水彩名家交流大展
　　　　　　「遊園尋夢」中正紀念公園園林之美水彩展

張明祺 Chang Ming-Chyi　1947

現職　恆安製藥有限公司總經理
　　　中華亞太水彩藝術協會準會員

學歷　大專畢業

獲獎　1980 臺灣恆安製藥有限公司總經理
　　　1992 貴州汎德製藥有限公司董事長
　　　1997 貴州傑宏塑料包裝公司總經理
　　　2003 南瀛藝術獎水彩類第一名（桂花獎）
　　　2004 屏東半島藝術季駐地藝術家獲獎榮譽
　　　　　　第57屆全省美展水彩類第一名
　　　　　　第4屆玉山美展水彩類第一名
　　　2004 年度南瀛藝術獎水彩類第一名（桂花獎）
　　　　　　第五十屆中部美展水彩類第二名

畫歷　2002 臺灣師範大學圖書館藝文空間個展
　　　2004 美國德拉瓦州立大學個展、基泰建設藝文空間個展
　　　2006 花蓮第一信用合作社藝文空間個展
　　　2007 臺中市文化局大墩藝廊（一）個展
　　　　　　屏東縣文化局第一藝廊個展
　　　　　　河海山林專題展（玉山國家公園）
　　　2008 紀念臺灣水彩百年當代2008水彩大展
　　　　　　「臺灣意象--櫻花鉤吻鮭暨雪霸百景」主題展
　　　　　　臺灣森林之美水彩巡迴特展
　　　　　　臺灣民主百景百位名家藝術聯展
　　　　　　塔塔加至玉山主峰步道之美水彩展
　　　　　　（玉山國家公園）
　　　2009「印象風城」水彩展
　　　2010「水彩的壯闊波濤」兩岸水彩名家交流大展
　　　　　　「遊園尋夢」中正紀念公園園林之美水彩展

范植正　Fan Chi-Cheng　1947

現職　台灣水彩畫協會會員
　　　台灣國際水彩畫協會會員
　　　中華亞太水彩藝術協會準會員
　　　松風畫會會員

獲獎　2001 經濟部綜藝展西畫組金牌獎
　　　2002 經濟部綜藝展西畫組入選
　　　2003 全省公教人員書畫展水彩類入選
　　　2004 中部美術展水彩類入選
　　　2004 經濟部綜藝展西畫組金牌獎及榮譽獎
　　　2005 全省美展水彩類入選
　　　2005 新竹美展水彩畫類優選
　　　2005 基隆市雞籠美展水彩畫類第一名
　　　2006 新竹美展水彩畫類佳作
　　　2006 台北縣美展油畫水彩畫類入選
　　　2006 基隆市雞籠美展水彩畫類佳作
　　　2006 南投縣玉山美展水彩畫類入選
　　　2006 經濟部綜藝展西畫組銀牌獎及榮譽獎
　　　2007 台陽美展水彩畫部入選
　　　2007 屏東縣屏東美展水彩畫類入選
　　　2007 新竹美展水彩畫類佳作
　　　2008 台陽美展水彩畫部入選
　　　2008 新竹美展水彩畫類入選
　　　2008 經濟部綜藝展西畫組銀牌獎及榮譽獎

畫歷　2009 范植正水彩畫個展─台灣電力公司彰化區處藝文走廊
　　　　　　范植正水彩畫個展─蕭如松藝術園區
　　　2010「遊園尋夢」中正紀念公園園林之美水彩展

林玉葉　Lin Yu-Yeh　1954

現職　個人工作室 教授繪畫
　　　台灣國際水彩畫協會會員
　　　中華亞太水彩藝術協會預備會員

學歷　國立台灣藝術學院畢業

經歷　1994-2008台北市建安國小美術資優班兼任教師

畫歷　1991 苗栗文化中心國畫個展
　　　1992 國立台灣藝術館國畫個展
　　　1993 台東社教館國畫個展
　　　1994 基隆文化中心國畫個展
　　　1995 美國休斯頓僑藝中心三人聯展
　　　1998 中正紀念堂懷恩藝廊國畫個展
　　　2002 中國湖南省長沙市、益陽市國畫聯展
　　　2004-2008 台灣國際水彩畫協會聯展
　　　2010「遊園尋夢」中正紀念公園園林之美水彩展

洪東標　Hung Tung-Piao　1955

現職　玄奘大學視覺傳達設計系兼任講師
　　　新莊社區大學
　　　台灣師大附中美術班教師
　　　中華亞太水彩藝術協會理事長
　　　台灣國際水彩協會常務理事

學歷　臺灣師大美術系畢業
　　　臺灣師大美術研究所碩士

獲獎　1979 師大美術系畢業美展水彩第二名‧油畫第三名
　　　1979 全國青年為寫生比賽第二名
　　　1980 三十四屆全省美展水彩獲台南市獎（第四名）
　　　1982 憲兵文藝金荷獎、新文藝金像獎（第三名）
　　　1983 全國美展水彩佳作獎
　　　1984 第三十八屆全省美展 省政府獎（第一名）
　　　1985 第三十九屆全美展優選獎
　　　1987 教育部文藝創作佳作獎

畫歷　歷任全國美展、高雄市美展、台北縣美展、新莊美展、寫
　　　生比賽之評審委員
　　　1980-2008 個展八次、應邀參加亞洲等國際聯展24次
　　　2005「十大名家畫帝寶」作品為名廈「帝寶」典藏
　　　2006「2006國際華人經典水彩大展」於歷史博物館一樓
　　　2006 應邀參展中國北京
　　　　　　「1905-2006中國百年水彩畫展」
　　　2007 國父紀念館百美圖邀請展
　　　　　　國父紀念館中山樓40週年百景邀請展
　　　　　　河海山林專題展（玉山國家公園）
　　　2008 台灣水彩一百年大展
　　　　　　紀念臺灣水彩百年當代2008水彩大展
　　　　　　臺灣森林之美水彩巡迴特展
　　　　　　臺灣民主百景百位名家藝術聯展
　　　2009「福山之美」水彩特展
　　　2009 台北植物園詩畫聯展
　　　2009「印象風城」水彩展
　　　2010「戰地鐘聲」馬祖列島百景大展
　　　　　　「水彩的壯闊波濤」兩岸水彩名家交流大展
　　　　　　「遊園尋夢」中正紀念公園園林之美水彩展

WONDERING
IN THE DREAMLAND
- THE BEAUTY
OF CHIANG KAI-SHEK
MEMORIAL PARK
中正紀念公園
園林之美

謝明錩　Hsieh Ming-Chang　1955

現職　專職水彩畫家
　　　國立台灣藝術大學美術系兼任副教授
　　　聯合報副刊專欄作家
　　　台灣國際水彩畫協會常務理事
　　　中華亞太水彩畫協會常務理事

學歷　輔仁大學中國文學系畢業

獲獎　1978 雄獅美術新人獎第一名，大專青年書畫聯展第二名
　　　1982 國家文藝獎（青年西畫特別獎）
　　　1983 全省美展第二名、青溪文藝銀環獎
　　　1984 全省美展第四名、北市美館當代水彩彩墨展第三名
　　　1986 中國文藝協會文藝獎章、全國美展金龍獎
　　　1987 教育部文藝創作獎第二名
　　　1988 中華民國畫學會金爵獎
　　　1997 著作《水彩畫法的奧秘》榮獲金鼎獎

畫歷　歷任全國美展、全省美展、各縣市地方美展、教育部文藝
　　　創作獎、公教美展、學生美展、青年寫生比賽之評審委
　　　員、個展至今十三次
　　　2003 應邀參展長流美術館
　　　　　　「台灣美術戰後五十年作品展」
　　　2003 入編文建會
　　　　　　《台灣當代美術大系媒材篇-水彩與素描》
　　　2004 獲選為70年代台灣鄉土美術代表人物之一
　　　2004 入編文建會《台灣現代美術大系-鄉土寫實藝術》
　　　2005 「十大名家畫帝寶」召集人
　　　　　　作品為名廈「帝寶」典藏
　　　2006 「2006國際華人經典水彩大展」於歷史博物館一樓
　　　2006 應邀參展中國北京
　　　　　　「1905-2006中國百年水彩畫展」
　　　2006 第十三次個展《隱藏的韻律系列》北縣文化局
　　　2007 為西德名鞋「勃肯鞋」繪製宣傳巨幅作品
　　　　　　「勃肯風雲」
　　　2007 擔任台北市立美術館美術作品典藏委員
　　　2008 《結構新美學》謝明錩第十四次個展台南格爾畫廊
　　　2009 「福山之美」水彩特展 、 台北植物園詩畫聯展
　　　2009 「印象風城」水彩展
　　　2010 「戰地鐘聲」馬祖列島百景大展
　　　　　　「水彩的壯闊波濤」兩岸水彩名家交流大展
　　　　　　「遊園尋夢」中正紀念公園園林之美水彩展

李招治　Li Zhao-Zhi　1956

現職　水彩藝術資訊雜誌專欄主筆
　　　中華亞太水彩藝術協會準會員

學歷　國立臺灣師範大學美術系研究所四十學分班結業

獲獎　1975 國父紀念館第三屆全國青年書畫比賽佳作
　　　1984 師大美術系畢業展國畫第二名
　　　　　　師大美術系畢業展書法第二名
　　　　　　師大美術系畢業展篆刻第二名
　　　2008 竹塹美展水彩佳作
　　　　　　雞籠美展水彩佳作
　　　2010 北縣美展全國組第三名

畫歷　2007 國父紀念館百美圖邀請展
　　　　　　國父紀念館中山樓40週年百景邀請展
　　　　　　河海山林專題展（玉山國家公園）
　　　2008 紀念臺灣水彩百年當代2008水彩大展
　　　　　　「臺灣意象---櫻花鉤吻鮭暨雪霸百景」主題展
　　　　　　臺灣森林之美水彩巡迴特展
　　　　　　臺灣民主百景百位名家藝術聯展
　　　　　　塔塔加至玉山主峰步道之美水彩展
　　　　　　（玉山國家公園）
　　　2009 「福山之美」水彩特展
　　　2009 台北植物園詩畫聯展
　　　2009 「印象風城」水彩展
　　　2010 「戰地鐘聲」馬祖列島百景大展
　　　　　　「水彩的壯闊波濤」兩岸水彩名家交流大展
　　　　　　「遊園尋夢」中正紀念公園園林之美水彩展

劉淑美　Liu Sue-Mei　1956

現職　個人畫室教授繪畫
　　　臺灣國際水彩畫協會會員
　　　中華亞太水彩藝術協會准會員

學歷　台灣藝術大學畢業

畫歷　2010 「水彩的壯闊波濤」兩岸水彩名家交流大展
　　　　　　「遊園尋夢」中正紀念公園園林之美水彩展

陳品華　Chen Pin-Hua　1957

現職　美術教師退休
　　　現任專業畫家

學歷　臺灣師大美術系畢業

獲獎　師大畢業美展水彩第一名
　　　第五屆南瀛獎水彩第一名
　　　第47屆全省美展水彩類第一名
　　　教育部文藝創作獎水彩類第一名
　　　21北市美展水彩類特優
　　　全省公教美展水彩類第一名

畫歷　2006「2006國際華人經典水彩大展」於歷史博物館
　　　　　　福華沙龍黃金秋色五人水彩聯展
　　　2008 紀念臺灣水彩百年當代2008水彩大展
　　　　　　臺灣民主百景百位名家藝術聯展
　　　　　　台灣水彩一百年大展於歷史博物館
　　　2009「福山之美」水彩特展
　　　2009 台北植物園詩畫聯展
　　　2009「印象風城」水彩展
　　　2010「戰地鐘聲」馬祖列島百景大展
　　　　　　「水彩的壯闊波濤」兩岸水彩名家交流大展
　　　　　　「遊園尋夢」中正紀念公園園林之美水彩展

李曉寧　Lee Hsiao-Ning　1959

現職　臺北市立明湖國小美勞教師
　　　中華亞太水彩藝術協會準會員

學歷　臺北市立師院美勞教育系畢業
　　　臺北市立師專音樂科畢業

獲獎　2005 新竹美展水彩類佳作
　　　　　　北縣美展水彩類佳作
　　　　　　南瀛藝術獎水彩類入選
　　　2006 新竹美展水彩類佳作
　　　2006 新竹美展工藝類入選
　　　　　　中華民國國際藝術學會美展水彩類優選
　　　2007 新竹美展水彩類入選
　　　2008 北縣美展水彩類全國組入選
　　　2010 玉山獎第二名

畫歷　2009 臺北市立社教館—「花影入簾間」水彩個展
　　　2009 臺北縣政府「縣府藝廊」水彩個展
　　　2009 臺北縣消防局「鳳凰藝廊」水彩個展
　　　2009「印象風城」水彩展
　　　2010「戰地鐘聲」馬祖列島百景大展
　　　　　　「水彩的壯闊波濤」兩岸水彩名家交流大展
　　　　　　「遊園尋夢」中正紀念公園園林之美水彩展

許德麗　Hsu Te-Li　1961

現職　台北縣立新埔國中教師
　　　中華亞太水彩藝術協會正式會員兼任理事
　　　水彩藝術資訊雜誌專欄主筆

學歷　國立台灣師範大學美術系畢業
　　　台灣師大美術研究所四十學分班結業

獲獎　2005 第五十九屆全省美展水彩第二名
　　　2006 第十七屆全國美展水彩入選
　　　2007 基隆美展水彩佳作
　　　2008 屏東美展
　　　　　　大墩美展入選
　　　2009 大墩美展水彩第二名

畫歷　2007 國父紀念館百美圖邀請展
　　　　　　國父紀念館中山樓40週年百景邀請展
　　　　　　河海山林專題展（玉山國家公園）
　　　2008 紀念臺灣水彩百年當代2008水彩大展
　　　　　　「臺灣意象---櫻花鉤吻鮭暨雪霸百景」主題展
　　　　　　臺灣森林之美水彩巡迴特展
　　　　　　臺灣民主百景百位名家藝術聯展
　　　　　　塔塔加至玉山主峰步道之美水彩展
　　　　　　（玉山國家公園）
　　　2009「福山之美」水彩特展
　　　2009 台北植物園詩畫聯展
　　　2009「印象風城」水彩展
　　　2010「戰地鐘聲」馬祖列島百景大展
　　　　　　「水彩的壯闊波濤」兩岸水彩名家交流大展
　　　　　　「遊園尋夢」中正紀念公園園林之美水彩展

遊園尋夢

WONDERING
IN THE DREAMLAND
- THE BEAUTY
OF CHIANG KAI-SHEK
MEMORIAL PARK
中正紀念公園
園林之美

程振文　Chen Cheng-Wen　1964

現職　專業畫家
　　　水彩藝術資訊雜誌專欄主筆
　　　中華亞太水彩藝術協會理事
　　　新竹市政府藝術顧問
　　　新竹市文化局藝術季審查委員

學歷　國立新竹教育大學美勞教育系畢業

獲獎　1998「百合」15屆全國美展水彩類佳作
　　　1999「紅與黃」竹塹美展水彩類竹塹獎
　　　2000「農村曲」63屆台陽美展水彩類金牌、台陽獎

經歷　1985-2007 個展共七次
　　　2001 新聞局"臺灣生態之美歐洲巡迴展"
　　　2002 國立交通大學"名家畫荷邀請展"
　　　　　 台北市生態藝術邀請展
　　　2007 海峽兩岸四地水彩畫邀請展
　　　　　 國父紀念館百美圖邀請展
　　　　　 國父紀念館中山樓40週年百景邀請展
　　　　　 河海山林專題展（玉山國家公園）
　　　2008 紀念臺灣水彩百年當代2008水彩大展
　　　　　「臺灣意象---櫻花鉤吻鮭暨雪霸百景」主題展
　　　　　 臺灣森林之美水彩巡迴特展
　　　　　 臺灣民主百景百位名家藝術聯展
　　　　　 塔塔加至玉山主峰步道之美水彩展
　　　　　（玉山國家公園）
　　　2009「福山之美」水彩特展
　　　　　 台北植物園之美詩畫聯展
　　　　　「印象風城」水彩展
　　　2010「戰地鐘聲」馬祖列島百景大展
　　　　　「水彩的壯闊波濤」兩岸水彩名家交流大展
　　　　　「遊園尋夢」中正紀念公園園林之美水彩展

林毓修　Lin Yu-Hsiu　1967

現職　國中美術教師
　　　中華亞太水彩藝術協會準會員

學歷　臺灣師範大學美術系學士

畫歷　2002-2007 新莊現代藝術創作協會年度會員聯展
　　　2006 中山樓百景聯展
　　　2007 國父紀念館百美圖邀請展
　　　　　 國父紀念館中山樓40週年百景邀請展
　　　　　 河海山林專題展（玉山國家公園）
　　　2007 人體素描個展---三峽老木林藝廊
　　　2008「2008臺灣當代水彩大展」聯展
　　　　　「民主百景」聯展
　　　　　 紀念臺灣水彩百年當代2008水彩大展
　　　　　「臺灣意象---櫻花鉤吻鮭暨雪霸百景」主題展
　　　2009「福山之美」水彩特展
　　　2009 台北植物園詩畫聯展
　　　2009「印象風城」水彩展
　　　2010「戰地鐘聲」馬祖列島百景大展
　　　　　「水彩的壯闊波濤」兩岸水彩名家交流大展
　　　　　「遊園尋夢」中正紀念公園園林之美水彩展

周嘉成　Zhou Jia-Cheng　1969

現職　插畫家
　　　中華亞太水彩藝術協會準會員

學歷　逢甲大學水利工程學系肄業

經歷　1996 聯合報插畫
　　　1997 中國時報插畫
　　　1997 自由時報插畫
　　　2007-2008 玄奘大學視覺傳達應用學系兼任講師

畫歷　2007 玉山國家公園「河海山林」美展
　　　2007 個展於老木林藝廊
　　　2008 臺灣的森林特展
　　　2009 個展於庶民美術館
　　　2010「戰地鐘聲」馬祖列島百景大展
　　　　　「水彩的壯闊波濤」兩岸水彩名家交流大展
　　　　　「遊園尋夢」中正紀念公園園林之美水彩展

鄧詩展　Teng Shih Chan　1969

現職　基隆市安樂區建德國民小學教師
　　　中華亞太水彩藝術協會准會員

學歷　國立新竹教育大學美勞系畢業
　　　國立台灣師範大學藝術研究所碩士

獲獎　第41屆全省美展水彩入選
　　　1986 年大專青年書畫展水彩入選
　　　1986 年全國青年水彩寫生入選
　　　1986 年高雄市美展水彩入選
　　　1987 省主席盃全國水彩寫生比賽第三名
　　　2005 年光華寫生社會組水彩佳作

畫歷　2006 國父紀念館「中山樓百景美展」
　　　　　　作品為國父紀念館收藏
　　　2007 玉山國家公園「河海山林」美展
　　　2008 國立台灣民主紀念館
　　　　　　「台灣意象-櫻花鉤吻鮭暨雪霸百景」專題展
　　　2008 國立台灣民主紀念館「臺灣當代2008水彩大展」
　　　2008 國立中正紀念堂「福山之美水彩展」
　　　2009 彰化市永豐銀行「鄧詩展作品展」
　　　2009「印象風城」水彩展
　　　2010「戰地鐘聲」馬祖列島百景大展
　　　　　　「水彩的壯闊波濤」兩岸水彩名家交流大展
　　　　　　「遊園尋夢」中正紀念公園園林之美水彩展

王瀚賢　Wang Han-Shien　1970

現職　台北市立松山工農美術教師
　　　中華亞太水彩藝術協會准會員

學歷　台北教育大學美術系畢
　　　台師大美術研究所碩士

獲獎　1984 塞拉耶夫冬季奧運海報設計全國預選特選獎
　　　　　　第一屆全國科學想像畫第三名
　　　　　　19屆全國青年水彩寫生大專組第三名
　　　1998 松山奉天宮水彩寫生比賽入選
　　　2006 信義區傳統藝術季水彩寫生社會組第一名
　　　2007 光華獅子會水彩寫生優選

畫歷　2005「飛躍的圖騰」聯展於蘇錦皆畫室
　　　2006 第二屆國立台灣師範大學研究生聯展
　　　2007 台北縣藝文中心光彩畫展三人展
　　　　　　基隆市文化中心浮影·畫痕三人展
　　　　　　玉山國家管理處河海山林聯展
　　　　　　國父紀念館中山樓之美聯展
　　　　　　國父紀念館之美一百美圖聯展
　　　　　　新店市立圖書館王瀚賢油畫個展
　　　　　　林業試驗所台灣的森林水彩展
　　　2008 紀念臺灣水彩百年當代2008水彩大展
　　　2009「福山之美」水彩特展
　　　2009 台北植物園詩畫聯展
　　　2009「印象風城」水彩展
　　　2010「戰地鐘聲」馬祖列島百景大展
　　　　　　「水彩的壯闊波濤」兩岸水彩名家交流大展
　　　　　　「遊園尋夢」中正紀念公園園林之美水彩展

曾己議　Tseng Chi-I　1972

現職　新莊高中美術班教師
　　　銘傳大學商業設計系講師
　　　中華亞太水彩藝術協會

學歷　國立台灣師範大學美術研究所碩士

獲獎　省公教美展水彩第一名
　　　北縣美展油畫水彩類第一名
　　　全國美展水彩第三名
　　　全省美展油畫類第三名
　　　南瀛美展水彩優選

畫歷　2000-2005 個展（師大畫廊、台北縣藝文中心）
　　　2005 半島藝術季駐站藝術家
　　　2006「2006國際華人經典水彩大展」於歷史博物館
　　　　　　福華
　　　2007 國父紀念館百美圖邀請展
　　　　　　國父紀念館中山樓40週年百景邀請展
　　　　　　河海山林專題展（玉山國家公園）
　　　2008 紀念臺灣水彩百年當代2008水彩大展
　　　　　　臺灣民主百景百位名家藝術聯展
　　　　　　台灣水彩一百年大展於歷史博物館
　　　2009「福山之美」水彩特展
　　　2009 台北植物園詩畫聯展
　　　2009「印象風城」水彩展
　　　2010「戰地鐘聲」馬祖列島百景大展
　　　　　　「水彩的壯闊波濤」兩岸水彩名家交流大展
　　　　　　「遊園尋夢」中正紀念公園園林之美水彩展

遊園尋夢
WONDERING IN THE DREAMLAND
— THE BEAUTY OF CHIANG KAI-SHEK MEMORIAL PARK
中正紀念公園
園林之美

吳冠德 Wu Guan-De　1979

現職　中華亞太水彩藝術協會正式會員兼任秘書長
　　　國立新莊高中美術班教師
學歷　國立高雄師範大學美術系畢業
　　　國立臺灣師大美術研究所碩士

獲獎　1998 全省文藝季寫生比賽第一名
　　　1999 第25屆全國青年寫生比賽高中組第一名
　　　2004 第32屆全國青年寫生比賽社會組第一名
　　　2007 獲台灣師大優秀研究生獎
　　　2010 台北縣美展第一名

畫歷　2007 國父紀念館百美圖邀請展
　　　　　　國父紀念館中山樓40週年百景邀請展
　　　　　　河海山林專題展（玉山國家公園）
　　　2008 生息 個展於新莊藝文中心
　　　2008 紀念臺灣水彩百年當代2008水彩大展
　　　　　　「臺灣意象---櫻花鉤吻鮭暨雪霸百景」主題展
　　　　　　臺灣森林之美水彩巡迴特展
　　　　　　臺灣民主百景百位名家藝術聯展
　　　　　　塔塔加至玉山主峰步道之美水彩展
　　　　　　（玉山國家公園）
　　　2009「福山之美」水彩特展
　　　2009 台北植物園詩畫聯展
　　　2009「印象風城」水彩展
　　　2010「戰地鐘聲」馬祖列島百景大展
　　　　　　「水彩的壯闊波濤」兩岸水彩名家交流大展
　　　　　　「遊園尋夢」中正紀念公園園林之美水彩展

蔡秀雅 Tsai Hsiu-Ya　1980

獲獎　1997 海中天寫生比賽 - 第2名
　　　1997 光華杯寫生比賽 - 優選
　　　1997 日本國際高校生比賽國畫類-入選
　　　1998 瓦磘溝觀光運河親水綠地創意徵圖比賽- 第2名
　　　1998 雙和美展 - 佳作
　　　2000 南投我愛河川水彩創作-入選
　　　2002 安徒生童話--插畫創作獎-入選
　　　2004 日本亞細亞水墨畫交流-特優獎
　　　2004 第3屆全國百號油畫展 - 入選
　　　2004 第2屆桃源創作獎 - 優選
　　　2005 第3屆桃源創作獎 - 入選
　　　2006『長頸鹿量身高』入圍金鼎獎
　　　2006『長頸鹿量身高』榮獲2006年好書大家讀

畫歷　兒童繪本類：
　　　2005 魔豆傳奇繪本兩本(日月文化)
　　　2006 長頸鹿量身高(格林)
　　　2007 美國文學Harcourt Achieve Anthology Explorer配圖
　　　2007 美國McGraw 教材配圖
　　　2008 小老鼠Piano 教材繪本繪製。
　　　廣告類、產品類：
　　　1999 領取-淡水街頭藝術家執照
　　　2006 麥當勞DM繪圖
　　　2007 統一企業-純喫茶-彩繪磁鐵瓢蟲
　　　2008 優莉瑪拼圖繪製-聖誕系列
　　　2010 約翰走路素描繪製
　　　　　　「遊園尋夢」中正紀念公園園林之美水彩展

劉庭豪 Liu Ting-Hao　1985

現職　中華亞太水彩藝術協會準會員
獲獎　2003 日本亞細亞水墨展佳作
　　　2005 台北縣美展水彩類佳作
　　　2006「行天宮人文獎」全國美術創作西畫成人組優選
　　　2007 第十二屆大墩美展水彩類優選

畫歷　2010「水彩的壯闊波濤」兩岸水彩名家交流大展
　　　　　　「遊園尋夢」中正紀念公園園林之美水彩展

羅淑芬　Luo Shu-Feng　1967

學歷　1985 畢業於新竹師專美術科
　　　1996 畢業於台北市立師院美術教育系
　　　2009 畢業於台灣師範大學美術研究所

獲獎　1982 新竹師專美術科校慶美展 工藝類組
　　　1983 參加台北市萬人寫生比賽大專組第三名
　　　1983 新竹市假日寫生比賽大專組第二名

畫歷　1987 全國公教美展 入選
　　　1987 高雄縣地方美展
　　　1987 彰化縣美術家聯展
　　　1989 全國公教美展 入選
　　　1988-1990 彰化縣美術家聯展(年度)
　　　2004-2007 擔任桃園縣花燈比賽評審員
　　　2004-2010 桃園縣美術協會年度展
　　　2009 中壢藝術館個展
　　　　　《向黃金比例致敬---羅淑芬的藝路探尋》
　　　2009 師大德群藝廊
　　　　　《權力慾望與性別演義---羅淑芬創作展》
　　　2010「遊園尋夢」中正紀念公園園林之美水彩展

郭心漪　Kuo Hsin-I　1974

現職　真工藝術負責人
　　　中華亞太水彩藝術協會準會員

獲獎　2009 大墩美展入選
　　　　　中華民國國際藝術美展優選
　　　　　玉山美展入選
　　　　　台灣美術新貌展入選
　　　　　兩岸秋季沙龍展新銳藝術家特別獎
　　　2010 中部美展第三名
　　　　　礦溪美展入選
　　　　　日本國際公募未來展入選

畫歷　2001 台中市文化局郭心漪師生陶藝成果展
　　　2002 台中市文化局陶藝與西畫個展
　　　2010 台中市文化局水彩畫個展
　　　　　英才文教基金會「郭心漪水彩個展」
　　　　　兩岸藝術家秋季沙龍新銳藝術家特別獎聯展
　　　　　「遊園尋夢」中正紀念公園園林之美水彩展

柯衛光　Ke Wei-Guang

現職　國立師範大學-生態藝術學程講師
　　　玄奘大學 視覺傳達設計系講師
　　　亞熱帶生態藝術協會常務監事
　　　中華亞太水彩藝術協會準會員

畫歷　1998 獲ECO－ART 生態藝術展〈太平洋建設獎〉
　　　1999 國際生態藝術展
　　　2001 台灣鳥類畫展
　　　2001 台灣生態之美
　　　2002 獲邀 行政院新聞局 台灣生態之美 歐洲巡迴展
　　　2002 國立教育館 生態繪畫、攝影展
　　　2003 獲邀 行政院新聞局-
　　　　　台灣生態之美 歐洲、非洲巡迴展
　　　2003 台灣生態之美聯展
　　　2004 玉山風華展
　　　2004 野地探索 聯展
　　　2005 寫實新象四人聯展
　　　2005 大地之美 聯展
　　　2006 台中由鉅畫廊 賀歲新春聯展
　　　2008 紀念臺灣水彩百年臺灣當代水彩大展
　　　2008 臺灣意象－櫻花鉤吻鮭雪霸百景藝術
　　　2009 自然香頌－台灣生態藝術特展
　　　2009 全球暖化藝術之眼－墾丁鳥類藝術特展
　　　2010「遊園尋夢」中正紀念公園園林之美水彩展

國家圖書館出版品預行編目資料

遊園尋夢：中正紀念公園園林之美 / 國立中正紀
念堂管理處，中華亞太水彩藝術協會作. -- 初
版. -- 臺北市：中正紀念堂，2010.10
　　面；　公分
　　ISBN　978-986-02-4726-8（精裝）

1. 水彩畫　2. 畫冊

948.4　　　　　　　　　　　　　　99018395

Book Title | Wondering in the dreamland - The beauty of Chiang-Kai Shek Memorial Park	書　名　遊園尋夢 — 中正紀念公園園林之美
Authors | National Chiang Kai-shek Memorial Hall, Chinese Asia Pacific Watercolor Art Association	作　者　國立中正紀念堂管理處、中華亞太水彩藝術協會
Issuer | Tseng Kun-Ti	發 行 人　曾坤地
Publisher | National Chiang Kai-shek Memorial Hall	出版機關　國立中正紀念堂管理處
Address: No.21, Zhongshan S. Rd., Zhongzheng Dist., Taipei City 10048, Taiwan (R.O.C.)	地　址　10048 臺北市中正區中山南路21號
Tel: 02-2343-1100　Fax: 02-2357-9655	電　話　02-2343-1100　傳真：02-2357-9655
Website: http://www.cksmh.gov.tw	網　址　http://www.cksmh.gov.tw
Artistic Director | Hung Tung-Piao	藝術總監　洪東標
Editor in Cheif | Liang Yung-Fei	總 編 輯　梁永斐
Editors | Chang Mei-Mei・Chen Cheng-Wen・Wu Guan-De	主　編　張美美・程振文・吳冠德
Excutive Editor | Li Tzu-Ying	執行編輯　李姿瑩
Writers | Chen Cheng-Wen・Hua Ping-Jung	撰　文　程振文・花炳榮
Collector | Ou Yang Wen Hui	資料彙整　歐陽文慧
Watercolor Works | Chinese Asia Pacific Watercolor Art Association	水彩作品　中華亞太水彩藝術協會
Illustrators | Lee Hsiao-Ning・Lin Yu-Hsiu・Chen Cheng-Wen	插　畫　李曉寧・林毓修・程振文
Photography | Hua Ping-Jung・Chen Cheng-Wen	攝　影　花炳榮・程振文
Works Photography | Liu Guang Zhi	作品攝影　劉光智
Art Design | redblackdesigns, Inc.	美術設計　朱墨形象設計廣告有限公司
Printing | redblackprinting, Inc.	印　刷　朱墨文化印刷事業有限公司
Address: 8F-6, No. 21, Sec. 6 Zhongxiao E. Rd., Nangang, Taipei, Taiwan	地　址　臺北市南港忠孝東路六段21號8樓之6
Tel: 02-2788-2000	電　話　02-2788-2000
Suggested Price | NTD 1,500	定　價　新臺幣1,500元
Publication Date | Oct 2010	出版日期　2010年10月
Edition | First Edition	版　次　初版
Sales Store |	展 售 處
National Chiang Kai-shek Memorial Hall	國立中正紀念堂管理處
Address: No.21, Zhongshan S. Rd., Zhongzheng Dist., Taipei City 10048, Taiwan (R.O.C.)	地　址　10048臺北市中正區中山南路21號
Tel: 02-2343-1100	電　話　02-2343-1100
www.cksmh.gov.tw	www.cksmh.gov.tw
Wunan Bookstore	五南文化廣場
Address: No.600, Jun Fu 7 Road, North Dist., Taichung City 40642, Taiwan (R.O.C.)	地　址　40642 台中市北屯區軍福7路600號
Tel: 04-2437-8010	電　話　04-2437-8010
www.wunanbooks.com.tw/wunanbooks/	www.wunanbooks.com.tw/wunanbooks/
Government Publications Bookstore	國家書店
Address: 1F., No.209, Songjiang Rd., Zhongshan Dist., Taipei City 104, Taiwan (R.O.C.)	地　址　104 臺北市松江路209號1樓
Tel: 02-25180207	電　話　02-25180207
www.govbooks.com.tw	www.govbooks.com.tw
ISBN 978-986-02-4726-8（Hardcover）	ISBN 978-986-02-4726-8（精裝）
GPN 1009902778	GPN 1009902778

指導單位 | 教育部　主辦單位 | 國立中正紀念堂管理處　承辦單位 | 中華亞太水彩藝術協會　協辦單位 | 瑞昱半導體股份有限公司・生展企業股份有限公司・國立新莊高中